Bible Codes Revealed

Bible Codes Revealed

The Coming UFO Invasion

Sherry Shriner

iUniverse, Inc.
New York Lincoln Shanghai

Bible Codes Revealed
The Coming UFO Invasion

Copyright © 2005 by Sherry Shriner

All rights reserved. No part of this book may be used or reproduced by any means, graphic, electronic, or mechanical, including photocopying, recording, taping or by any information storage retrieval system without the written permission of the publisher except in the case of brief quotations embodied in critical articles and reviews.

iUniverse books may be ordered through booksellers or by contacting:

iUniverse
2021 Pine Lake Road, Suite 100
Lincoln, NE 68512
www.iuniverse.com
1-800-Authors (1-800-288-4677)

ISBN: 0-595-33559-4

Printed in the United States of America

I dedicate this book to Jehovah, the Most High God. May He be glorified and exalted and His truth proclaimed among the nations.

Contents

Introduction 1

Chapter One   In the Beginning… 9

Chapter Two   Faction 3 and the Alien Agenda 16

Chapter Three   To Serve Man: The Aliens are Coming
and They're Cannibals! 21

Chapter Four   Aliens Will Overthrow America 24

Chapter Five   The Difference Between Fallen Angels, Demons,
Aliens, Jedi, and the Watchers 34

Chapter Six   The Prisoners of Dulce Base 47

Chapter Seven   Planet Rahab—Lucifer's Seat.
Was there another planet in our solar system that
disappeared? What happened to it? 56

Chapter Eight   Mars: What's Really Going On
and What They Won't Tell You 63

Chapter Nine   Planet X, Sedna and Toutatis—Signs in the Sky—
The Armies of the Antichrist 68

Chapter Ten   NESARA: The Political Agenda of the Beast 79

Chapter Eleven   The Two Beasts of Revelation 13:
The Antichrist and The False Prophet 95

Chapter Twelve   Tearing Down the NWO Strongholds:
Orgone As A Self Defense Weapon 110

Chapter Thirteen   The Kingdom of God 118

Chapter Fourteen Tell Them The Prophesied Time Has Come 128

Conclusion 139

Websites Run By Sherry Shriner 141

How To Make Orgone Blasters 143

Acknowledgments

To my website readers from over 116 nations of whom many encouraged me to put this information in book form. To Ann Cooper who made this book possible. To all of those who have supported my online ministry and work for the Lord and my Internet talk show including Marie, Posey, Patricia, Kristine, Del, Elliott, and Arron from Australia. To Zeph Daniel for his friendship and insight. May the Lord bless you all. To my parents who instilled in me a love for the Lord and Bible Prophecy at a very young age. To Ronda Zeoli, my right hand, and to Angie who have both always been there to encourage and support my work for the Lord online. To Paul Palomba who spent many hours editing this manuscript. And To my husband and kids who I love very much. I praise the Lord for you all.

Introduction

It would stand at the foot of my bed and stare at me as I lay trying to sleep. Fear and sheer terror would grip every muscle and bone I had. It was at least 7 feet tall, dark, and evil. It wore a pitch black cape that completely covered its body from head to toe. I would shrivel under my blankets and pray for it to go away. I did not know what it was other than feeling it was some evil being straight from hell and I certainly did not know what it wanted.

Night terrors are real.

I continued to be haunted throughout childhood of this evil, demonic being scaring me at night. Often I would also see other shorter, creepy, black shadows move throughout the room whenever I was trying to sleep. I was too scared to move or even breathe for that matter. Going to sleep for me would mean to close my eyes and keep them closed just so I did not have to look at them however I could always feel their presence when they were around. I developed a keen sense to know when demonic beings were around me even if I could not see them and yet I did not know how to get away from them or what to do about it. I would just pray for the Most High to protect me.

Later in life, I would learn as an adult that the tall one was one of Lucifer's generals sent to kill me. I did not know who they were, but these beings knew who I was. From the time I was born, Lucifer knew I had a prophetic calling on my life, and that as an adult, I would grow up to become one of his arch enemies. I would learn as an adult how to expose, attack, and tear down his strongholds that he would create to control and destroy mankind. To prevent this from happening, he had assigned one of his top ranking generals to kill me.

Lucifer is on a mission to control the world as the Antichrist. I am on a mission to make it as miserable as possible for him. I despise him.

My mission started by being born to a God fearing family in Cleveland, Ohio during the winter of 1965. From my earliest childhood memories, I cannot remember a time when I did not know who Jesus was. I have loved Him since I can remember. When I was two years old, I was proclaiming His Name. I would become re-born in Him at the age of five. My life has been a journey from wondering how to become closer to Him to learning and building that close relationship that no one could ever replace. My true love in life was and has always been God Himself.

As time passed, I was enrolled in private Christian schools and had attended church almost every Sunday during the 18 years I lived with my parents. But as I was growing up through churchianity or simply the system of religion, I always felt there was something missing. I was miserable and I could not figure out why.

Although I loved Jesus, I hated religion. There was just something wrong with the whole thing, and I could not put my finger on it at the time. Out of 100,000 plus denominations, by luck, I had landed in the denomination that had everything right, and everyone else was wrong. Yes, I am being sarcastic.

But for these reasons, I have always been a nonconformist, and it has been an uphill battle to be forced to live in a world of conformity. As a child, I was the black sheep, the rebellious one who would not conform and believe what I was told to believe simply because I was supposed to believe it. I knew there were doctrinal errors in the churches, which was clear from a young age. I had found my own mind. I had my own views and my own thoughts, and I was determined to keep them even if they had to stay my own. And yet at times, I did not even know where they were coming from or why I had them.

By the age of 12 I had read the Bible from front to back, being partial to the book of Revelation. Not fully understanding much of the book, the beast rising out of the sea with 7 heads and 10 horns fascinated me. By the age of 18, I had probably read the Bible more times than most pastors and had repeatedly read several of the Old and New Testament books.

I became an avid student of Bible prophecy. I could not get enough of hearing about end time events, the arrival of the Antichrist, and ultimately, the Second Coming of Jesus Christ. It was also during those early pre-teen years that I had read my first Bible prophecy book which I had taken off my dad's bookshelf. Reading Hal Lindsey's *Late Great Planet Earth* not only changed my life, but seemed to give me direction. I identified with it, and it seemed to define who I was and who I would later become. As I read the pages of end time events, I knew I would be involved in these events and that I would be a warrior in the last days for the Most High God.

Bible prophecy has always had a strong hold over my life. I can not escape it. I was born for these last days. I was born to be a warrior. For this reason Lucifer had targeted me as a child for death. He had sent his forces to intimidate me and keep me from discovering my relationship with Yahweh or from achieving what I was destined to become. He didn't succeed then, and he still hasn't. And every day I live, I use to fight against him and the kingdom he is trying to establish here in some way.

From the first time I had heard about the Second Coming of Jesus Christ, I was hooked. That is all I cared to hear about. That is all I wanted to hear about. Nothing else about religion interested me much. I had seen enough and experienced enough of it daily to know religion itself was hypocritical. Religion was a road paved with good intentions but rarely traveled correctly by anyone on it. Most people in the churches just seemed pretentious and fake and more centered around man, materialism, and gossip circles than God Himself. And to question theology and beliefs was almost blasphemous to them. By typical churchianity standards, I was certainly going to go to hell if I didn't believe everything the church taught and the way they taught it.

I also learned at a young age that other people didn't experience quite the same things as I did. Looking back, I can now see that I was just more in tune with the spiritual world than anyone else I knew. Of course, as a child, you wouldn't know what that was. So I learned to keep things to myself and not talk about the things that scared me or the monsters I saw or felt near me. The mere mention of monsters was sure to bring fits of hysterical laughter from others. And it always did.

As I grew up, the beings from hell never went away. They were always stalking me, but I no longer feared them either. I learned that by calling on the Name of the Lord, they would leave, and if they did not I just ignored them. If I moved, they followed. When I was in college, I didn't notice them much, if at all. I do not know if they went away or if I was just too busy to notice. It seems back then, I never just went to bed. I simply passed out from exhaustion. It was when I was in college at Liberty Baptist University in Lynchburg, Virginia that I began a career in radio news. I became the campus radio news director after my first year. During that time, I landed my first job at a radio station in Lynchburg, Virginia as a political news reporter and announcer. At the same time, I also served as an intern political correspondent with a competing station under an alias in Roanoke, Virginia. I was having fun. It had been a long time dream to have a career in television news broadcasting. Radio would be a way to break into it and give me experience and a chance to build my resume. My experience at Liberty University culminated with several journalism awards.

After two years in Virginia, I transferred to Kent State University where I was elected to become the director of their campus radio news department. During that time, I also took a job with a local newspaper focusing on political news. I graduated in 1991 with degrees in Criminal Justice, Journalism, and Political Science.

Shortly after graduating, I moved to Washington D.C. and found there were not any doors opening for me at all. I had my eyes set on the Washington bureau of CNN. The Atlanta bureau had suggested with my political news reporting experience that I get into the Washington bureau. However the Washington bureau said I did not have enough experience. I was going in circles and without any real options. I decided to move back to Ohio and got married shortly after. It was not too long after that when I realized "**they**" were back. And it was then that I finally just had enough of them. It was time to find out who they were and why they were stalking me.

I was married, unemployed, had my first child, and was finally staring reality in the face. It was time to confront who these demonic beings were and what they wanted with me.

I embarked on an intense research over the next 5 years into spiritual warfare, hell, demons, Satan, and continued into my favorite areas of end time events and last days prophecies. I studied the deception in the churches, UFOs, government black operations, the New World Order, and much, much more. I went into many different areas and began to learn that the faces of our government and military were much different from their backsides. At the same time, I started to research and learn about spiritual warfare, something the churches just seem to ignore. I learned about hell, and demons, and how to fight against these forces. I went to war against the general, and his forces assigned to me, and I haven't seen them since. We have power in the Name of Jesus to cast demonic beings into the abyss, and once I learned that, it can became quite an easy task to just kick anything evil around me into the abyss.

As a result, I began to pray daily that the Lord would show and teach me what He wanted me to learn and know. I would ask Him to teach me the truth in all things and to reveal the mysteries of His kingdom to me. And I still pray this almost daily.

My research would culminate over the years into an enormous journey of unraveling conspiracies and lies in our government and churches. Five years turned into ten and I just kept going and have not stopped since. In 1994 I would begin to have visions from God and did not recognize what they were. It would take me a long time to realize that the strange things I were seeing were visions from the Lord Himself.

From this experience, I learned that it takes the heart of a truth seeker to really get to know Yahweh. As you start abandoning and letting go of preconceived ideas and beliefs and realize all the error of being spoon fed by dogma and religion, only then can He teach you, but not until you stop telling Him what the truth is with your words and your actions. And that is what I had to learn, to let everything go, and let Him teach me from the ground up. I had to build my foundation just in Him and on Him and not from my own self obtained knowledge or what man had taught me.

Most importantly, during this time, I learned how to have the one thing that I had always felt missing, an intimate relationship with Yahweh Himself. I learned the difference between having head knowledge of Him and heart knowledge of Him. I learned what it was to go into the proverbial wilderness with Him and just sit at His feet and learn who He is and how to hear His voice. He then became, and still is, my main source for information. If I want to know something, I ask Him. I seek Him direct for the answer. I get up every day and I ask Him to teach me the truth in all things and to reveal the mysteries of His kingdom to me. I ask Him to lead and guide my thoughts. I have learned what it truly means to be walking in His Spirit. Being in His Spirit does not mean speaking in gibberish that is not from Him. It means becoming one with Him in Spirit by seeking Him and walking with Him and learning how to hear His voice and recognize His leading and how He works. When you learn who He is, you learn what He is not, allowing the deceptions around you to be magnified and exposed for what they are. You can see them, recognize them, and know what is or is not of Him.

There is nothing special about me. I just love Him, and I am committed to Him. As He continued over the years to give me visions and prophecies and reveal future events to me, I began to create websites revealing the information I learned through Him and from His leading. Today I have 12 websites on the Internet, and a blogger and as the days come to a close I am busy fulfilling my calling and destiny in Him. I have worked hard building and maintaining websites over the years to educate and inform His people to what has gone on, is going on, or what is coming, and I won't stop until He says it is time to. And as my enemies can attest, I can not be intimidated either. I have received several death threats over the years and have posted some of them on my websites out of amusement. Mostly, I ignore them. I do not fear Lucifer, and certainly, I do not fear man. The Lord is my strength.

In 2001, I was led by the Lord to buy a Bible Codes program and learn how to search for and analyze codes. I had no idea what I was doing, and it was very complicated to learn. There were many times I wanted to just give up, but He would keep me at it, and He began to show me how to operate the program, how to look up terms, and how to analyze what I was finding. In essence, He basically taught me how to decode the Bible Himself. I learned how to decode my own name and I confirmed that the Lord had anointed me to decode His Word, I learned more about my calling in Him and who I was, and why I was born. I learned that I was His messenger, an emissary and a mouthpiece for Him in these last days. I was called to be a Watchman, a Prophet, and a warrior for Him. The Lord even told me and then showed me in His records that I was King David's grand daughter.

When He revealed this to me in 2004, things began to make sense. For years Yahweh would always tell me I reminded Him of David. One day He said to me, "You remind Me of your grandfather." And I asked, "Which one?" And He said, "David." When He said that, I was not just shocked. I was completely floored! I had seen royalty terms all over my Bible Code, but I had no idea I was related to King David. He told me to go into the codes, and I would find it. Sure enough, I did.

The codes also explained the boldness and lack of fear I had developed in fighting against Lucifer and his new world order. As my ancient grandfather King David fought the giants in his day without fear, I too had stepped forward to fight against the giants in these last days without fear. I had come a long way from being a child who would hide under her blankets.

Without God's anointing and direction, I do not even think it is possible to get very far in understanding or decoding Bible Codes accurately. It is very difficult and not something you can even do without discernment. Sure, there are those who try to decode and even publish their results but I have found very few that are really led by Him to do them. Most interpreters decode out of their own interest and curiosity and make a multitude of mistakes.

Finding a Bible Code is half the battle. You have to know how to accurately read and analyze the information and understand how the Hebrew language uses terms. Without the Lord's anointing and key to decoding, I would not be the decoder I am today. He has given me a key to the codes. When He told me He had given me a key to the codes, I did not really understand the extent of what He had said until I saw the work of many other decoders and their little if not complete lack of understanding of how the codes really work.

Over the years, God has revealed to me through the codes His records and the plans of mankind. I have learned how to use the codes to unravel daily events and find the truth in them about what is really happening and in the process, expose the media and government lies that are being told to the public. I have also learned how to expose the events that are planned for the future by Lucifer, including the organizations, governments and secret societies working to bring him into power. One thing is certain, the government lies and uses the media as a mere tool for their deceit. And it has been my experience that being an accurate decoder makes a person a prime target of their surveillance.

In 2002 the Lord specifically led me into what I have termed the Alien Agenda and has revealed much information to me about the coming UFO and Alien invasion to America and our Earth. He has shown and continues to show me different routes being taken to spearhead the arrival of end time events and what they really are, as opposed to what the churches and prophecy gurus teach. The Lord has shown me and led me to expose the plans of those who are involved in the various groups within governments, which are unified around the world and competing against one another to bring Satan to power as the Antichrist. More importantly, He has shown me how to tear down their strongholds.

In 2003, the Lord told me "You will speak to the Nations." The Lord is using me to wake up, warn, and teach His people about coming events and has said, "Lead My people back to Me," which has become my mandate and one of my messages to the world today. Come back to the Most High God!

In 2004, He proclaimed, "I am raising you up as a Prophet to the Nations." Today over 116 countries visit my websites on a daily basis, and as of this writing, over 100 countries are listening to my internet radio show at http://www.sherrytalkradio.com As an internet radio show host, I expose the Luciferian New World Order, UFOs, Aliens, the Alien agenda, the coming UFO invasion, Planet X, NESARA, the deceptions in the churches, and the coming of the Antichrist to power. Other than with Him at my side, I do it almost alone.

Personal donations help me cover the costs of my websites and radio shows, but I do not have webmasters to design or run my websites, nor do I have a radio producer to prepare my shows or help me put them together, nor can I afford to pay for them. I am just a voice in the wilderness who He has called to stand up against the strongholds of the devil and the New World Order in these last days.

I have several venues in doing this, and I am using every one of them to wake up God's sleeping people and sound the alarms concerning what is coming.

It has become evident you will not learn the truth in the churches today. The cycle of error and deception has continued through every age since Constantine and the Council of Nicea in 325A.D. Most churches today are graveyards for the spiritually dead. It is the churches that are the "Whores of Babylon" and it is America who is modern day Babylon.

Furthermore, most people are clueless concerning what will really happen in the last days and even regarding Yahweh Himself. They do not understand how to have a real relationship with Him because they have allowed their churches to take the place of Him, and they simply do not know how to seek Him. They think reading the Bible and praying is all they need to do, and in this book, I am going to open your eyes as to how you can have a more intimate relationship with Him. Jesus said the last days would be as the days of Noah. The problem is that most churches do not teach nor realize what those days were really like. It was an Alien Agenda then, and it is the same one now, but I am going to reveal what the Lord has shown me and what is really going on behind the scenes in our world today. If you believe our country is one nation under God, prepare to be shocked.

The aliens from the past have hidden themselves from the public view. Nevertheless, they are ready to come back into dominance in these last days as the armies of the Antichrist. Eventually a full blown invasion will occur, and it is coming sooner than you think. The rise of the Antichrist is around the corner. Have the governments and the churches of the world been secretly working together to bring him to power? Have they worked together to suppress and silence prophets of old such as Enoch so those today would not recognize the aliens for who they are?

When you are done reading this book your eyes will be opened to the truth that the Lord has revealed to me.

Chapter One

In the Beginning…

In the book of Genesis we read that in the beginning the earth was without form and void of where there had once been a thriving civilization, it had been obliterated out of existence.

Signs of earlier life would be found thousands of years later such us batteries, air craft, and microwaves. These artifacts indicate extreme intelligent life had once existed before ours and pre-dated well before the flood of Noah. So much so that our own modern technologically advanced world could not even begin to explain how a civilization before ours could have been so much more advanced than our own.

Religion tried to squelch inquiries as if such truth seeking was not of God, or even necessary. They did not have the answers about this previous civilization. And if they did, they did not want someone else outside of their control providing them. Perhaps, they were keeping the past as secrets of their own. Science could not, or would not, offer valuable explanations either. Science has never been capable of explaining the spiritual, but it is the spiritual that can define and explain science.

Digging into the Bible Codes, I discovered there was indeed a thriving technologically advanced civilization on earth previously and that because of their rebellion against the Most High, its civilization was obliterated out of existence, causing the complete destruction of the earth.

This civilization on earth contained the ancient cities of Atlantis and Lemuria and had inter-galactic trade with other planets such as Mars, Venus, and the others within our solar system. When Lucifer rebelled against the Most High as the reigning cherub over all these planets, he instigated a multi-planet rebellion bringing the Lord's wrath of hailstones of fire against all the planets involved.

Entire angelic civilizations were destroyed, and many of these angels involved that did not face His immediate judgment of imprisonment were forced into the hollow areas of their respective planets to survive.

The Bible speaks of Lucifer's rebellion in Isaiah 14:12-14

> "How are thou fallen from heaven, O Lucifer, son of the morning! How art thou cut down to the ground which didst weaken the nations! For thou hast said in thine heart, I will ascend into heaven,I will exalt my throne above the stars of God: I will sit also upon the mount of the congregation, in the sides of the north: I will ascend above the heights of the clouds; I will be like the most High
>
> In Ezekial 28 it says: You were the anointed cherub that covers, and I had put you in the holy height of God...

Lucifer was not happy just being a high ranking cherub with rule over several planets. He wanted to be like the Most High God. And you will find the pre-Adamic, pre-historic civilization on this earth within his realm of dominion and rebellion.

Most of us are led to believe that Lucifer's rebellion was a quick event that was quickly put down by the Most High God, but it did not happen that way.

The Lord said to me, "You pray for My mysteries and I am revealing them to you." So what I am going to reveal is not something I have spent an incredible time on or research, and perhaps I will later for my websites, but for now in a nutshell the Most High has revealed to me that during the early pre-Adamic civilization, also known as the prehistoric civilization it was a time of angelic attempt to create man and animals.

The evolutionists were not completely wrong. These things did exist at one time, a concept the church refuses to even acknowledge. But where everyone has gone wrong is in who created what.

Lucifer's rebellion was when he recruited 1/3 of the angels to attempt to be Gods with him as the leader, or "Most High." In doing this they were trying to create perhaps themselves. The angels we know are spirits, but they are humanoid. They are human looking and they do have bodies, not all of them are pure ethereal spirits. But the angels could never get it right. If you look at Neanderthal, the Cro-Magnum and the other types of what we refer to as cave men or ape men, they could never accomplish what the Most High would with mankind. And that is why the evolutionists cannot find the missing link. The link between the ape looking creatures of prehistoric times and the humans we have today were not related nor created by the same hand of the Most High.

They also attempted to create their own animals, and that is where we got the dinosaurs and other odd creatures we see in mythology and folklore. The skulls and bones of prehistoric man and animals have been found from this ancient time when Lucifer and his followers, the angels who followed him, were trying to create their own world. We don't know what types of animals they had here to begin with, nor do we know exactly what types are in heaven now, but there were animals of some kind, and it was these beings that the angels crossbred into the mythological creatures we have heard about such as the mermaid, unicorn, dinosaurs etc...

Atlantis and Lemuria were cities on Earth where these angels dwelled and developed technology that far surpassed anything we have ever had or seen. And they were not confined to earth, they could travel to distant planets and visit, trade, and cohabitate with the angels who lived on them. In fact, the New World Order is nothing but this ancient planetary old world order revived for the last days. Planetary trade and economics was Lucifer's dominion, and he ruled from a distant planet called Rahab. The Bible codes reveal that Lucifer had a mansion or dwelling place on all these planets including earth, but his home planet was Rahab, located between Mars and Jupiter, and it was completely destroyed and cast out of our solar system with its inhabitants imprisoned inside of it. Rahab is returning to earth in these last days and is known more commonly as Nibiru or Planet X where those imprisoned will be released and allowed to come to earth to help Lucifer subdue and conquer it. When the Lord judged and destroyed Rahab He allowed Lucifer and some of his forces to escape.

The DNA imprint of humans is 11-22-33 and the angels couldn't duplicate it. It represents the 11 ribs, 22 bones in the skull, and the 33 vertebrae of mankind. To this day, these are the most significant numbers for any occult group in existence. They could not figure it out then, and to this day, they cannot master and duplicate Yahweh's creation of man and woman.

After the Most High had had enough of their rebellion, and having given them plenty of time to repent for doing so, He utterly destroyed their homes and civilizations. The planets were all destroyed with hailstones of fire, and those who rebelled were cast into imprisonment or forced to make homes in the inside hollow cavities of their respective planets to live in. As part of their judgment, they lost their angelic looks and appearance and became ugly grotesque looking beings.

When the Most High recreated the earth, many, perhaps thousands of years later, Lucifer and his minions watched. And they conspired to destroy the creation of man and woman that Jehovah had placed in the Garden of Eden.

Since the recreation of earth and the creation of Adam and Eve, Lucifer has worked behind the scenes directly and indirectly conspiring and working to destroy the Most High's plans. And since Lucifer's initial rebellion, the Lord has allowed it and used Lucifer for His own purposes through it all.

> Isa 45:7 "I form the light, and create darkness: I make peace, and create evil: I the LORD do all these things."

Lucifer has been and always will be inferior to the Most High. A created being can never be greater than the Creator. Yet he has been working for the past several thousand years for the prophesied time when he will be allowed to come to earth and rule for 42 months. Lucifer is serving the Most High's plans to test mankind. Will mankind serve and follow the Most High or choose to follow the lies and deceptions of Lucifer?

During pre-Adamic times, Satan deceived 1/3 of the angels as a high ranking Cherub to rebel against the Lordship of the Most High, and it led to their judgment and destruction. In these last days, he will be allowed to rise on earth once again, this time as the Antichrist. He will incarnate man and come announcing he is Jesus and receive mankind's worship that he is God deceiving those on the earth once again.

He has been busy planning and preparing over the centuries how he will come to power. As the prince of the air, he has been ruling within the first and second heavens, as he and his millions of fallen angelic forces have been watching and conspiring how to take over the world. Can our government stop it? Can a global government uniting all the world forces together stop it, or are they simply part of the plan?

It was during the 20th century when the fallen angels, known now as aliens, would discover deep caverns in North America and start to infiltrate the underground, subterranean world under the United States. As the United States began building deep underground bases, the aliens saw how they could manipulate these for their own uses and began to make contact with military and political officials. Our earliest records are of a treaty they made with President Roosevelt in

1933. It was William Cooper, a former navy intelligence officer, that would blow the lid on the contact our government had had with aliens in "Behold A Pale Horse."

Soon after the release of his book, others would step forward with information and documents of agreements made with these aliens that our government had made with them. Information was provided by former underground base security guards, engineers, and scientists who worked in these bases. It was these bases such as the Dulce Base in Dulce, New Mexico and Area 51 in Nevada that were products of the treaties signed with the aliens. For they were constructed and built to become joint alien and human underground bases where technology could be exchanged between the aliens and humans as agreed upon in the treaties signed with them of which I will get into more detail of later in this book.

Lucifer and his forces probably recognized America as the Great Babylon prophesied of in Revelation 17 and 18, and they set out to infiltrate it so they could overpower it and rule over it. Their stepping stone into our society was their bribes of technology. They would teach our government how to create and fly their own anti-gravity aircraft among other things. In exchange, our government would conceal their presence here and allow them to abduct animals and humans for their own purposes.

What they probably did not expect was the eventual dominance the aliens would have in our skies and under our earth. UFOs are presently everywhere, some just watching the people on earth, some abducting people or mutilating animals. What is getting more and more obvious is that their presence can no longer be contained.

After having met some of these aliens former president Franklin Roosevelt demanded "In God We Trust" be imprinted on all the currency of the United States. In 1963 one conspiratorial reason for the assassination of President John F. Kennedy was because he wanted full government disclosure to be given to the public on aliens from other worlds visiting ours. In 1984 former president Ronald Reagan tried to muster congressional support for a Star Wars Initiative Self Defense Program. What is it these men knew that propelled them? What exactly scared them to come forward to attempt some kind action against an alien presence, or even threat, to our country and world?

Although much information has been uncovered about joint alien and human underground bases, space stations, and projects, beware of the disinformation that will come out as a result. In the future, as now, many will come out proclaiming the "truths" of aliens in our midst. However, not everything they say is true. The real purpose is to push a dark hidden agenda and to hide the real truth.

Many of the lies being told today is for this specific reason: Lucifer is pushing his agenda to be accepted as God on earth in stages. One of the ways he is doing it is to have his forces pose as Ascended Masters and speak to humans through what is known as channeling to inform the public on the paranormal, occult, UFO's, earth changes, and to HERD and BRAINWASH the people into believing Aliens from outer space are our Forefathers and Creators.

They are creating the foundation for the biggest deception that has ever been perpetrated on mankind.

They want us to believe that mankind is a creation of these aliens and that they are our gods, and therefore there is no real God. The Bible will be wrongfully discredited, and it will be proclaimed that there are no such things as natural God given rights.

These aliens are not extra terrestrial beings from millions of miles away or other galaxies. There are some which occupy distant planets and stars but they are mostly subterranean. They live within both earth and parts of our solar system. They did not create us. They created the ape man and cave men who no longer even exist. All were destroyed in judgment. The Bible explicitly tells us that Satan is the prince and the power of the air. It tells us about demons, hell, hybrids and the Nephilim and Annunaki. It also tells us how Satan came back to corrupt earth after its recreation and will eventually be worshipped as the god of this world.

Satan was the cause of the earth's previous destruction, and he will be the cause of it again as we race into the last days prophesied in the Book of Revelation and other passages of Scripture. He will once again attempt to cause the entire earth to rebel against the Most High God and use his puppet associate the Bible refers to as the False Prophet to demand the world worship him as God.

I see two different scenarios that can be played out here: In the first one, Satan will have pawns arrive here on earth claiming to be Messiahs and even one claiming to be Jesus before Satan will arrive himself as "God." The second scenario is that he just arrives himself claiming to be the promised Messiah, and then the world worships him as God. The armies of aliens coming will claim they are our forefathers and creators as per the plural term "Elohim" mistranslated in the KJV, and they will serve as the armies of Satan to help him subdue, conquer and control the earth.

The fallen angels, after seeing what the Lord created in Adam and Eve, never stopped trying to mimmick that creation; however they could never succeed either. We read in the book of Enoch, and I will get to that in later chapters, how a second rebellion among the Most High's angels would occur, and they would come to earth to physically cohabitate and reproduce with humans. This would replace their own bioengineering attempts at creation, and they would physically be able to produce children with human women. When the Lord eventually destroyed that rebellious attempt with a Flood and drowned them all, this did not stop them, however, as they would return to impregnate human women (Genesis 6:4) and much later during our century turn to test tube creations, cloning, and soul scalping. And that is where we are today with their attempts to create their own human or 'master race' to outdo Yahweh's creation and be capable of producing and creating their own. And that is what they are doing in underground bases all over the world today and even in our space stations that have been well concealed from the public.

While millions of Lucifer's forces have continued with building their own master race plans, Lucifer has been involved with the political and economic systems of the world and has created secret societies to work together to bring him into power through a one world government.

What they call, the **New World Order.**

Chapter Two

Faction 3 and the Alien Agenda

When President Bush used the Gulf War 1 in 1991 to announce The New World Order, most people did not really know what he was talking about. Unity? Peace? Not a bad thing. But 'good will toward men' is not what he was talking about. His cunning grin, sleight of speech, and the usual political jargon and games played at the public's expense was going to be nothing more than the demise of the people he was claiming to bring peace to in this New World Order.

The New World Order is in itself a vast conspiracy of old bloodline families. The wealthy, the famous, the corporate elite, the United Nations, and the Secret Societies. Broken up into two factions better known as the Rothschild and the Rockefeller factions, it consists of double agents. Members switching factions, lies, betrayal, murder and general mayhem are the status quo among these who fight to gain control of the once secret hidden agenda to unite the world under a one global government to be ruled by one man. The winner gets all. The various countries of the world have agreed upon the plan, but no one seems to agree as to whom gets to rule it.

Watching it all from their aircraft and bases, infiltrations of government jobs, appointments, cabinets, Congress, the Pentagon, and even the White House, have been the subtle, yet consistent presence of aliens in our midst.

They are everywhere. And they are watching. From sabotaging missiles as they sit in silos to taking out a satellite or a rover here and there, they are eavesdropping on military bases, hanging out outside The White House, and even your house and mine. They are in the sky; they are on the ground, and they are infiltrating society as hybrids. The aliens aren't coming. They are here.

Would you recognize an alien if you saw one? Probably not right away. They use holographs to look human. Occasionally, you will hear of a story buried in a

Tabloid, or somewhere on the internet of people seeing others shapeshift in front of them or turn into an alien with scaled hands or skin. There are two different types of infiltration into a society.

The first way is direct breeding. You've heard of alien abductions, the little grey men abducting people into their UFOs, performing medical experiments on them, and then sending them back. There are the victims who do not remember all of the details. Some just remember seeing a UFO and then cannot explain for missing time. Some are taken repeatedly. Some are taken so often, they begin to empathize with their abductors. These stories are the same across the country and around the world without regard to age, race, or sex.

The second way the aliens infiltrate society is indirectly through the first way. Many abduction victims are being used as breeders. When they are taken, they become part of the alien breeding program, never realizing they may have had a role in donating eggs or sperm to the alien population agenda. Some women are impregnated, watched, and then the baby is taken at about 8-12 weeks. The woman has a mysterious miscarriage she cannot explain which defies medical explanation.

Some women will not even know they were pregnant to begin with. So, being a baby carrier for 8 or 12 weeks is not noticed because they take it out before you realized you were pregnant. These babies grow up in foster homes, or perhaps with the aliens in underground bases. Many women have successfully carried to full term, babies that they thought were their husbands or significant other's when the baby had an alien father. The mother never even knew it. These first generation alien hybrid children rank either above normal, as in star children, or do not rank at all, just quietly assimilating into society, passing their alien DNA on for generations.

In the days of Noah, mixed human and alien DNA was dominant. The iron mixed with miry clay that the Prophet Daniel spoke of were the wheat and the tares. It was so dominant there was only one family left with pure DNA, Noah's. That is the real reason God destroyed the world with a flood and started over. However, in Genesis 6:4 it says that even after the flood, the mixing of human and Alien DNA started yet again. And from that time, it has never stopped. Yahweh said the last days would be as the days of Noah. So today, even today, we have generations and lineages of alien DNA mixed with our own. Most of us have some form of alien DNA and do not even know it.

Having this alien DNA does not take away from the fact that you are a created soul. You are still human, you just have polluted DNA, and Yahweh already promised us He would never destroy the entire world again with a flood. In fact, the reason He comes back to the destroy world at all is because He promised He would return for those who believe in Him. And those who don't? You are on the losing side, and you might want to consider your options. Another fact is, even though Yahweh knew our generations would be mixed, He still proclaims today to many of His Prophets that He saved His best people for last.

There are many, many different races of these fallen angels. There were separate planets and nations of them before the fall. After the fall, multitudes were imprisoned inside the hollow cavities of their respective planets, while others were allowed to roam free. These are the ones we are dealing with today.

While factions of alien groups have been busy with breeding programs, others have been busy infiltrating our governments and secret societies. The Reptilians are the most notorious and well known among the bloodline families, who, after all, have their bloodlines linked directly to them.

These bloodline families are so protective of their lines that they even insist on intermarriage only simply because through their DNA, they can activate it to become hosts of Reptilians. Through this specific DNA, secret rituals, and blood drinking, those with this DNA can then invite and host a reptilian to possess them. This allows for shape-shifting. It also gives the Reptilians control of human bodies to work out of, from, and through. Human one minute, a Reptilian the next. A tall, scaled, lizard-type being. Think it's too far fetched to be true? I bet you've heard of werewolves. It's the same type of shape-shifting, only by lizards. And yes, it happens.

Some of these Reptilian-Human shape-shifters can be caught in between shifts; some turn green; some peoples face start to contort for no known reason, and you think you are seeing things. Most notable features of these shape-shifters are their beady snake eyes, or their long jaw bones, big noses and small eyes. Some have that wide-awake look, like their eyes are going to pop out of their heads.

Once you know what to look for even watching a state of the union address from the capital can be amusing. When I see the beady eyed ones, I half expect forked tongues to start spewing out of their mouths. Sometimes you will just see peoples grey hair start to look green for no apparent reason. Or they look like they are ready to jump out of their seats, all big-eyed like they have invisible toothpicks holding them open.

These are just some of the features that Yahweh has taught me to look for. The features of these hard core Lucifer loyalists who want to bring you their New World Order with themselves ruling this planet.

Granted, many of those people hosting reptilians, the most powerful Alien faction and dominant force on earth we are dealing with, reside in the other two factions. The third faction is a collective grouping of various other alien nations fighting for control. However, even in this one, the Reptilians are dominant. Why? Because the greys are slaves to the Reptilians. Futhermore the most powerful and hated grouping of aliens today are the greys, reptilians, mothmen, and draconians. All four are a collective nation to themselves. Lucifer, Satan, is a winged draconian. This is the nation with the agenda to dominate and rule earth, the third faction of the New World Order.

As a result, we have little grey beings with huge black eyes, most notable for their breeding agenda and human abductions. These reptilians look like large scaly lizards or sleestack, for those who remember that old Saturday morning show, "Land of the Lost." Mothmen are most notable for their red beady eyes and wings, not to mention their infamous appearance in West Virginia and their ensuing portrayal in the book and movie, "The Mothman Prophecies," while the Draconians are most notable for their portrayal in the Star Wars series. The Draconian look like Darth Vaders. Very tall, very black, caped, and hooded beings that never show their faces. Some call them Phantoms. Others just look like dragons. This is the group fighting for control of the New World Order and of which keeps threatening a literal UFO invasion of the earth.

This is the collective group the government makes treaties with one minute, then furiously spends billions of dollars on space defense programs the next in hopes of forming some kind of defense against them, such as H.A.A.R.P., space based scaler beam weapons, and others I am sure we have not even heard of. Government programs which are so black, you would never know they existed.

In addition, Faction Three is the group the Lord has led me to expose and inform the world of. Their existence is real; it's here; it's in space, and eventually they will be running the world with Satan, i.e. Lucifer, soon to be known as the Antichrist, or "messiah of the world" depending how gullible you are. He is not a messiah, and he is not **the** messiah. He is Satan posing as a messiah, and he is going to come to earth in a spectacular light, sound, and UFO show as he slowly descends to earth with the eyes of the world looking upon him.

So what does it come down to? Factions one and two are doing all the work in preparing the world for a global government, known as the New World Order, and when it's done, Faction 3 will step in and take control of it. There is nothing the others will be able to do about it.

Not a thing.

In Revelation chapter 13, the Apostle John wrote of the coming last days events and the plans of the Antichrist to rule the world with his pawn and puppet, the False Prophet forcing the entire world into beast/Satan worship. There will be worldwide Satanism. In order to participate in the new global economy, every person will be forced through various governments legislations to accept a chip or mark of some kind in or on their right hand or forehead. By accepting this chip or mark, one is also announcing their loyalty to the Antichrist and the acceptance of his world rule over this new economic system. The entire world will be forced to worship him as God.

Do not get the chip.

Do not get the mark.

Escape the coming enslavement by accepting Jesus Christ, Yahushua, as your Savior now before it's too late. For once you accept this chip or mark, you will forfeit your soul to Satan. You will spend eternity in hell with him once you die.

Chapter Three

To Serve Man: The Aliens are Coming and They're Cannibals!

Consider this: A warning of the future from the past given in a short episode on TV in 1962.

An alien visits the earth. He says they've come as friends, and they desire to help the earth and set up reciprocal visits to their planet. The aliens have noticed that the earth is plagued by both natural and un-natural calamities, and they only wish to help. They offer a new power source, an end to famine, and a force field to be used as a defense shield. The alien states, "We wish only that you simply trust us." As he departs, he leaves a book behind.

At this point, the decoding experts for the U.S. government go to work. A man named Chambers is part of a team assigned to translate the book, which turns out to be a most difficult task. While he is discussing the situation with several army generals, his assistant Pat rushes into the room with news that the title of the book has been deciphered. The title reads To Serve Man.

Meanwhile, the delegates at the UN watch a film of several tests given to the alien. It's basically a lie detector test, and the results show that the Alien is making truthful statements. He repeats his motive of coming to earth only to offer help. The countries of the world offer their thanks as deserts become gardens and armies are disbanded. Next we see people standing in line to board spaceships as the reciprocal flights to the Alien's planet begin. They are weighed upon entry, and speak of upcoming events as we would speak before embarking on a vacation.

Chambers and his assistant, Pat, discuss all the recent events. They note that there are no more codes to decipher, that nearly 2000 Aliens are now on earth, and how easily man decides to go off to a strange planet. In fact, they are both on a waiting list to go. Although Chambers has given up on deciphering the book, Pat states that she is still working on it and getting close to a translation.

Chambers is now in line to board the spaceship. As he is ascending the steps, Pat rushes up desperately trying to get his attention. As she is held back by the Aliens, she warns Chambers, "Don't get on the ship! The book, To Serve Man, IT IS A COOKBOOK!" A struggling Chambers is forced into the ship.

Chambers is taken to a solitary room. He is offered a meal, but he tosses it on the floor. An Alien enters the room, picks up the meal, and gives it to Chambers stating, "Eat. We would not want you to lose weight."

Chambers faces the camera and speaks directly to us.

He says, "Whether we are on the ship with him or back on earth, it does not matter; we will all be on the menu.

I could not say it any louder. We will all be on the menu!!

This was a short episode of the Twilight Zone played back in 1962. You can read about it at http://members.cox.net/kaiotea/serveman.htm

Most people are going to just think, well what do you expect from the Twilight Zone. When I read it, all I could think of was, how prophetic.

I have been sounding the alarms for over two years now that the aliens are not our friends. They are hostile carnivors, I refer to them as cannibals out of preference since when they are not trying to possess humans they eat them. And when they do invade the earth, there will be plenty of famine here because of the natural disasters and wars that happen before their arrival. And yes, mankind will be on their menu.

According to the Center for Exploited and Missing Children, over 300,000 children per year are missing. That does not include adults. And other than this being mentioned on a milk carton it's quietly swept under the rug away from the public's eye. The aliens aren't going to come to eat humans, they already are. It will just get worse when they arrive and there is no food to feed them. They will feast openly on humans, human body parts, and yes, this will happen in America.

The Lord has told me over and over that it will be a time of sheer terror, and the things that I have seen will cause exactly that, sheer terror. This illustration on the Twilight Zone, in fact, gives meaning to some of the things I've already seen about what is going to happen. Sometimes truth is stranger than fiction.

Unless you are found without guile in Yahweh and counted as worthy to escape all these things, you could indeed be a recipe in the alien's cookbook.

And they cannot wait To Serve Man.

Chapter Four

Aliens Will Overthrow America

Over the last year, the Lord has been showing and revealing to me the overthrow and destruction of the United States of America. It's been a sombering realization that nothing is going to happen exactly the way I've always been conditioned by the churches and prophecy gurus to believe. In fact, nothing could have prepared me for this other than being led into the Alien Agenda by Him several years ago.

Right now there are Reptilians in the White House, Draconians in the Vatican, and Greys in our skies abducting people around the world to use in breeding experiments, and for many, even eating them. Measures our government has agreed to cooperate to with these evil twisted beings to keep these things silent and has funded disinformation and discredited campaigns, projects, magazines and organizations to keep the truth from ever being discovered. Which is why, today, the official denial of the existence of UFO's and aliens is, in fact, an official denial. In exchange, they've reaped alien technology through black operations and have carved out of the earth underground joint human and alien bases where this exchange of technology and learning takes place. All funded by the tax payers.

The Stealth bomber, laser surgery, even the microchip are all "benefits" of trading humans for technology. 300,000 missing children each year, add missing adults, and the number would probably double. Our government has allowed approximately 600,000 American citizens to become victims of the Greys and UFOs every year since 1954 and have agreed to stay silent about it and deny it's happening all for the promise of technology. Don't you feel safer now? That is 30 million Americans alone. Now imagine this as a worldwide problem, because it is. Even if they wanted to, our government could not stop them, but they could inform the people instead of murdering those who have tried to get this information out to the public.

The whole reason of refusal about public disclosure of the alien problem is that neither the government nor military want to be part of the blame or finger pointing, so official denial it stays. What will they do when these Aliens decide they've had enough of tinkering with agreements and humans and just take over our world? And it's not if they will, but when. That is the part of the equation no one sees coming. America, the Alien Nation, will literally become an Alien Nation.

The Bible says "they will mingle themselves with the seed of men," and also in Daniel, we are warned of iron mixed with miry clay that will not cling to one another. It is impossible for those created and made in God's image to cling to those who simply want to destroy them and aren't even human. This last kingdom, the prophesied fourth and terrible beast kingdom that will arise in the last days, is an alien nation. For now, they roam earth awaiting their chance to destroy and kill mankind in their envy and rage for mankind being made in God's image. Soon the Lord will take His hand off of America and lift the veil allowing them to reveal themselves.

The presence of Aliens is nothing new to planet Earth. They have been here for thousands of years. Their Biblical identification is one of being fallen angels who rebelled against God and were kicked out of heaven. Their most notable name is Annunaki or Anuk.

Who were the Annunaki? They were the Watchers, Watchmen assigned to earth to watch over Yahweh's creation on earth. They were created by God as perfect angels. These Watchers rebelled against God and a mutiny followed as they lusted after human women and abandoned their mission to oversee humans and began to defile the women of the earth by having offspring with them.

> "When men began to increase on earth and daughters were born to them, the divine beings saw how beautiful the daughters of men were and they took wives from among those that pleased them…It was then, and later too, that the Nephilim appeared on earth—when the divine beings cohabited with the daughters of men, who bore them offspring. They were the heroes of old, the men of renown." (Genesis, Chapter 6, from the Jewish translation of the Torah.)

According to the Bible:

> "Now it came to pass, when men began to multiply on the face of the earth, and daughters were born to them, that the sons of God

(fallen angels) saw the daughters of men, that they were beautiful; and they took wives for themselves of all whom they chose…"

"There were giants (Nephilim) on the earth in those days, and also afterward, when the sons of God came in to the daughters of men and they bore children to them. Those were the mighty men of old, men of renown (Gibborim)." Genesis 6: 1-4.

"And the angels who did not keep their proper domain, but left their own habitation, He has reserved in everlasting chains under darkness for the judgment of the great day…having given themselves over to sexual immorality and gone after strange flesh (human), are set forth as an example, suffering the vengeance of eternal fire." Jude 6 & 7.

"For God did not spare the angels who sinned, but cast them down to hell and delivered them into chains of darkness, to be reserved for judgment; and did not spare the ancient world, but saved Noah, one of eight people, a preacher of righteousness, bringing in the flood on the world of the ungodly…" 2 Peter 2: 4-5.

The first Watchers who instigated the rebellion were judged accordingly. 200 Watcher officers, each in charge of tens of thousands of Watcher soldiers, abandoned heaven to mingle with earthly women. Even after the flood, many more rebelled and came to earth following their footsteps. These ones have not been judged yet. The bulk of these fallen angels from both of the earlier rebellions, Lucifer's and the Watchers, have been imprisoned in the hollow planet of Rahab, aka Planet Nibiru, which is now returning to earth to help Lucifer overthrow and dominate the earth in the last days. It is in these last days that the Lord will allow them to be released from their prison to fulfill their end time prophetic role in helping Lucifer subdue the earth.

In the Sumerian language, the term Annunaki meant "from heaven who came to earth."

The Annunaki had children that became known as the Nephilim, Rephaim, Emim, Gibborim, Philistines, Zamzummim, Anakim, Ivvim, and a few other names. The mixing of genes started with Cain's daughters, the women of Cainnan who created a DNA defect called giantism. Their children were giants. Some were 30 feet tall. Aliens are not demons. Demons are the spirits of the dead giant hybrid children.

These Watchers came to earth to be kings, emperors, priests, shaman, tuitongas, manitous, pharaohs, gods, and goddesses. They are the titans, pans, gods, goddesses, and fawns of Greek and Roman mythology. They have supernatural strength, psychic powers, and, often times, have six fingers and six toes. They want us to believe mythology is merely fiction, but it is not. Almost all of the characters are based on real Watchers or their hybrid children who played those roles while on earth. Yes, a lot of it is dressed up to make these characters heroes and gods and goddesses, but you can glean some real truth concerning what was going on back then, minus the garbage they threw in to make them all nice fairytales.

The Anuk are known to be shapeshifters and cannibals. They sacrifice humans, drink blood, levitate objects, astral travel, report the future, practice magical arts, and teach the art of war. They are the masters of astronomy and astrology. They taught mankind abortion so that they could keep certain women beautiful for sexual pleasure.

> **They** are the incubus and sucubbus. They are the magi of ancient Egypt and Babylon. They place and remove curses.
>
> **They** use poison, gossip, backbiting, and intrigue to take power and overthrow the true sons of God.
>
> **They** are master builders and built the ancient cities.
>
> **They** are the Atlanteans.
>
> **They** are half fallen angel and half human being.
>
> **They** are the Gibborim, mighty men of renown like Hercules the Titan.
>
> **They** are the stock that the antichrist will come from.
>
> **They** are fully fallen hosts and fully man.
>
> **They** were here before the flood and AFTER.
>
> **They** are the creators of the alien hybrid greys and UFOs of modern times.
>
> **They** are the seed of Satan. See Genesis 3:15 "And I will put enmity between thee and the women, and between thy seed and her seed; it shall bruise thy head, and thou shalt bruise his heel."

They can shapeshift into reptilian form and then back into their own.

They can be 7-9 feet tall on average.

They are the armies of the Antichrist.

They are the inhabitants of hollow Nibiru

They will be enforcers of the mark of the beast.

And as the Lord has told me, "Mens hearts will fail with fear when they see these beings on the earth." This earth is going to be cluttered with the tall, the ugly, and the damned. And it's coming sooner than you think!

Yahweh has given me visions in the Spirit of the fear and terror which will take place as these giant Anuk return to earth via Nibiru (and just rise up from their underground hideouts) and overthrow America and then the world.

At first, they may appear friendly, sincere, and offer to help earth struggling to survive from wars, natural catastrophies, and famines to deceive the world to invite them to our planet. But the facade of friendliness will not last.

They will overthrow our government, replace the law of the land, and dominate this land as they walk through it putting all people in subjection and fear of them. In America there will be millions of these giants along with the hordes of unhuman looking aliens of every shape and size and grotesque features that were part of Lucifer's rebellion who lost their angelic looks as part of their judgment.

There will be riots and uproars. People will run for their lives and try to fight against them. Sheer panic and the horror over this dominate and massive alien presence will sweep across America. Martial law will be declared, and those who fight against the aliens and the NWO will be terminated.

They will be everywhere, wicked and evil. They will force mankind here in America to commit unspeakable sins and atrocities and kill those who refuse without a second thought. They are not coming as our friends. They are complete haters and enemies of mankind who will make Americans their slaves.

They will walk through our neighborhoods, towns, and cities in every state and hunt the believers of Yahweh. They will enforce the mark of the beast. They will help Lucifer take physical control of the earth. They will maim, kill, rape, imprison, and terrify humans everywhere around the globe. As famines escalate because of natural catastrophies and wars, they will eat humans as prey.

Yahweh told me this:

Tell Them!

Do you see the picture developing? The last days are TERROR! WOE!

Woe to those who will seek to harm My little ones! My own I will protect, but Woe to the planners of evil and those who plan to destroy the world!

I will allow it and then MY Judgment will come!

Many pieces to the puzzle, I will show them to you and reveal My Glory through you to the nations.

My child, know this that the last days are of suffering and terror. Such terror has never been known before, those of old (Anuk) will walk and control the earth. They will commit and enforce evil of every kind. And when I return there will be more of them than man left. Woe! Woe!

Give them the warnings of terror to come so that they will find peace and strength in ME. For I shall lose nothing given to Me. Those in MY hands ARE MINE.

Many will be tested but they are MINE. To be refined in the fire and then set gloriously in MY light.

Tell them child. Tell them no one can even begin to imagine the horrors that are coming. Your safety and refuge are within ME!

TELL THEM!!

The mixing of fallen angel/alien with human DNA led to a giantism defect in the DNA of the hybrid offspring and an eventual, almost complete, contamination of, not only the human DNA, but the animals as well (beastiality was common). By the time Yahweh destroyed the world with a flood because of this contamination and to destroy the hybrid giants and deformed animals, only one family on earth was left with pure human DNA. But even after the flood, the Watchers kept revolting, and even more were punished and cast out of heaven, losing their first estate and habitation as they continued to defile women and human DNA. At the time Israel left Egypt, they had to conquer some 20 cities of the Watchers giant children to reclaim the land of Israel as their own. The Watchers were known as the Nephilim, Annunaki, or the heroes of old, men of renown as mentioned in Genesis 6:4.

Over the years, the human hybrid giant races were destroyed through wars and by their own corruption. The mixing of alien and human DNA did not vanish, it just went underground. Most humans today have contaminated blood in their DNA. Although the human hybrid giantism defect was perfected, the original Anuk are still giants.

This hybridization and corruption of the human DNA is still today very much a part of our world, and most hybridization goes undetected. It never stopped from the beginning; they just perfected it, creating their own human/serpent seed lines to mingle with humans. So why is the church silent on UFOs, Aliens, abductions, implantations, and forced breedings?

These Annunaki are not our creators. You can read in Enoch chapters 6-15 how they were created beings by Yahweh in heaven and were assigned to watch over the earth. When they rebelled, they were cast out of heaven, their first estate, although they do still reign in the first and second heavens and inhabit other planets and star systems visiting Earth in UFOs.

Many of them live in underground hideouts here in the earth. In the following years, the Theory of Evolution will be discredited from the very founder, supporters themselves, and their pawns. You can see this happening even now. They will then promote through Government Disinformation Scientists that mankind was created in a test tube by these Annunaki and that these Annunaki are our creators.

This is part of the grand delusion and lie at the end of the days. And we are in the end of the days.

Instead of preaching the truth, our churches changed the truth to lies and preached the "Sons of Seth" façade, changing the truth of Scriptures. These angels were the Sons of God who rebelled against Him. Our churches also sat back and allowed the Book of Enoch to be taken out of the Scriptures. What this did was hide the worldwide hybridization and the truth concerning who these aliens are and what they are doing.

Why? To keep people in the dark and unprepared for the great lie that is coming. They could not pull it off if everyone already understood who these aliens really are. Many pastors today are following the drumbeat of their training seminaries and not God. They are following man's wisdom, not God's while religious leaders aren't preparing their congregations for what is coming, and in their own ignorance, they do not even realize they've been deceived themselves because they refused the truth as it is in Yahweh, and they have blindly accepted only what man has told them to believe or teach.

The Lord has told me that in the coming days, these Aliens will make their presence more visibly and physically known on earth. They seek only to destroy mankind. Right now they are infiltrating many groups and organizations and claiming through gullible people to be ascended masters who want to help mankind. Do not believe their lies. They speak with forked tongues. They say they want to help save the earth while they plan its overthrow and destruction at the same time.

The veil is being lifted.

In the near future, even more than there are now, many people will start to proclaim the truths of aliens in our midst. However, not everything they say is true. Their real purpose is to push a dark hidden agenda and to hide the real truth. They will even televise worldwide an interview with an "alien" who is nothing but Satan himself in Alien form.

Many of the lies being put out is for this specific reason: To inform the public on the paranormal, occult, UFO's, earth changes, and to herd and brainwash the people into believing that the Aliens from outer space are our creators, our forefathers, ascended masters, and enlightened ones.

They are creating the foundation for the biggest deception that has ever been perpetrated on mankind. That mankind is a creation of these Aliens and that they are our gods, and therefore, there is no real God; the Bible will be wrongfully discredited, and they will proclaim that there are no such things as natural God given rights. It is about World Government and total control over the surviving masses by the elite of the occult secret societies. And that is what these incremental brainwashers will try to do.

These Aliens are not extra terrestrial; they are terrestrial and subterranean. They live within our earth and parts of our sky. The Bible explicitly tells us that Satan is the prince and the power of the air. It also tells us about demons, hell, hybrids and the Nephilim and Annunaki.

As the end of times approach, the lies of extra terrestrial lineage, heritage, and alien creation will come out in full force. It is up to you to reject these lies and cling to the truths of the Bible that God is our creator. Don't be deceived by them. Arm yourself with the Word of the Lord.

Yahweh gave this message to me:

It Is Time

Those not sent by Me will come against you round about. They will surround you on every side. Know this child, that I am with you. I will use you as My messenger to all who seek the truth and they will mock you and scorn you as they did Me.

The time is coming when the true servants of Mine will be here no more, taken up to be in My glory. Yes child, the time is coming.

Arm yourself with steadfastness and truth. Be bold in Me and My ways, do not look to the left or to the right, but in Me.

You shake the gates of hell and knock the walls down of great societies and kingdoms. Expose their plans as I reveal them to you, reveal everything I give to you My child and let Me handle your enemies. For they are great, but I AM Greater.

Do not sorrow child for those who refuse My instruction. Leave them in My hands and continue to do what I lead you to do. I have given you a sword and great anointing, look to Me and I will lead.

The sins of the world will be destroyed in one day, you will be with Me for eternity. Regain your strength in Me and continue on, for the time is short.

I Love You My child, and daughter of David, stand against the Giants and do not waiver. It is time.

I feel much urgency even writing this. The time is coming closer and closer when the USA will be invaded by thousands, perhaps millions of UFOs, armed and ready to overthrow our government and population. Our military will be defenseless against them. They will not come as friendly beings from outer space but as hostile enemies.

Naturally, the Aliens themselves have been working through the different factions, secret societies and world elite to bring about the NWO and global government. They puff up and promise leadership roles, fame and fortune in the coming global kingdom for those who cooperate with them now and help bring it to pass. But they will learn soon enough why Lucifer-Satan is called the Father of Lies. He will betray and kill them all when He rises to power. Do these people really think he would share his 'kingdom' with anyone?

Murder, mayhem, betrayal, double crossing, and an Alien invasion. Some of us understand the agendas taking place to form a one world government. Now take it a step further, as to who and what is really going to run the show. An agenda so hideous, the churches will not tell you and cannot because the real truth has been kept hidden from the public: **The Alien Agenda**

The time clock for America is ticking. Can you hear it as loudly as I do? The Lord is Warning America today. The Aliens ARE coming. The veil is being lifted and the Alien Nation beast kingdom, prophesied by Daniel and John, will come to pass enabling the Alien beast kingdom to take over the whole world.

If you are fence sitting, it's time to get off the fence. If you are backsliding, it's time to get back with Yahweh. Time is running out, and unless He protects you, there will be no place to hide. The only safety we have is in Him.

Chapter Five

The Difference Between Fallen Angels, Demons, Aliens, Jedi, and the Watchers

In these last days, the Bible says it will be a time of mass hybridization and the mixture and corruption of human DNA by fallen angels, also known as "Aliens."

The government is and has been, conditioning the existence of aliens through Hollywood, science fiction, cartoons, and other sources. However, they are not telling you the whole truth.

These Aliens are not ascended masters, or enlightened ones, or beings from galaxies millions of miles away, nor are they our forefathers or original creators. They are fallen angels who were kicked out of heaven for their rebellion against the headship of God, and they believe they have one last chance to try to usurp His authority. They know He is coming to the earth to destroy them once and for all, (Battle of Armageddon) and to gather those who are His and to establish His reign on earth.

The Lord has told me that in the coming days, these Aliens will make their presence more visibly and physically known on earth.

As the end times approach, the lies of extra terrestrial lineage, heritage, and creation will come out in full force.

Two Separate Rebellions in the Early Days

Most people are familiar with the rebellion of Satan wanting to be like God and wanting to be worshipped as God. For his sins of rebellion and pride, he lost his rulership over the planets he resided over and lost his place in heaven as a high ranking cherub.

What most people do not realize is that the rebellion of Satan's, leading 1/3 of the angels to try to usurp God's authority, and the rebellion of the Watchers are two separate events.

The Watcher's were not a part of Satan's rebellion; they created their own rebellion against God by deciding to leave their first estate which was heaven, and go to the earth to cohabitate with human women. Why doesn't the church ever address this issue? In fact, why did they try to cover it up by leaving Enoch out of the canon version of the Bible, and then manipulate the meaning "sons of God." They mistranslated Sons of God, (angels of God) creating some ridiculous theory suggesting it to mean Sons of Seth. People bought that explanation because they did not realize there was such a huge difference in changing that text around and it would keep them from the truth and allow the churches to cover it up.

Enoch was one of the greatest Prophets of God to have ever walked the Earth. In his lifetime he wrote 365 books. We have one of them. Where are the others? Are they lost or being kept hidden? It is in Enoch where we first learn about the rebellion of the Watchers, the angels assigned to watch over and guard over the earth:

In Enoch

Chapter 6:1 it says...

1   And it came to pass when the children of men had multiplied that in those days were born unto them beautiful and comely daughters.

2   And the angels, the children of the heaven, saw and lusted after them, and said to one another: 'Come, let us choose us wives from among the children of men

3   and beget us children.' And Semjaza, who was their leader, said unto them:

Enoch then continues to discuss a deal Semjaza makes with fellow Watchers to all commit the same sin.

In verse 7, it says that there were 200 chiefs on the summit of Mount Hermon, which is located on the border of Lebanon and Syria and stands over 9,000 feet high. They agreed to come to earth and cohabitate with women.

These 200 chiefs were each in charge of tens of thousands of other Watchers. So how many fell with them. We do not know, maybe they all did. That would put the number into the hundreds of thousands that fell from heaven and came to earth.

Chapter 7

1   And all the others together with them (this indicates their armies did follow them) took unto themselves wives, and each chose for himself one, and they began to go in unto them and to defile themselves with them, and they taught them charms

2   and enchantments, and the cutting of roots, and made them acquainted with plants. And they

3   became pregnant, and they bare great giants, whose height was three thousand ells: Who consumed

4   all the acquisitions of men. And when men could no longer sustain them, the giants turned against

5   them and devoured mankind. And they began to sin against birds, and beasts, and reptiles, and

6   fish, and to devour one another's flesh, and drink the blood (cannibalism). Then the earth laid accusation against the lawless ones.

Chapter 8

1   And Azazel taught men to make swords, and knives, and shields, and breastplates, and made known to them the metals of the earth and the art of working them, and bracelets, and ornaments, and the use of antimony, and the beautifying of the eyelids, and all kinds of costly stones, and all

2   colouring tinctures. And there arose much godlessness, and they committed fornication, and they

3   were led astray, and became corrupt in all their ways. Semjaza taught enchantments, and root-cuttings, 'Armaros the resolving of enchantments, Baraqijal (taught) astrology, Kokabel the constellations, Ezeqeel the knowledge of the clouds, Araqiel the

signs of the earth, Shamsiel the signs of the sun, and Sariel the course of the moon. And as men perished, they cried, and their cry went up to heaven.

Chapter 9

1 And then Michael, Uriel, Raphael, and Gabriel looked down from heaven and saw much blood being

2 shed upon the earth, and all lawlessness being wrought upon the earth. And they said one to another: The earth made without inhabitant cries the voice of their cryings up to the gates of heaven.

3 And now to you, the holy ones of heaven, the souls of men make their suit, saying, "Bring our cause

4 before the Most High. And they said to the Lord of the ages: Lord of lords, God of gods, King of kings, and God of the ages, the throne of Thy glory (standeth) unto all the generations of the

5 ages, and Thy name holy and glorious and blessed unto all the ages! Thou hast made all things, and power over all things hast Thou: and all things are naked and open in Thy sight, and Thou seest all

6 things, and nothing can hide itself from Thee. Thou seest what Azazel hath done, who hath taught all unrighteousness on earth and revealed the eternal secrets which were (preserved) in heaven, which

7 men were striving to learn: And Semjaza, to whom Thou hast given authority to bear rule over his associates. And they have gone to the daughters of men upon the earth, and have slept with the

8 women, and have defiled themselves, and revealed to them all kinds of sins. And the women have

9 borne giants, and the whole earth has thereby been filled with blood and unrighteousness. And now, behold, the souls of those who have died are crying and making their suit to the

gates of heaven, and their lamentations have ascended: and cannot cease because of the lawless deeds which are

10 wrought on the earth. And Thou knowest all things before they come to pass, and Thou seest these things and Thou dost suffer them, and Thou dost not say to us what we are to do to them in regard to these.

Chapter 10

1 Then said the Most High, the Holy and Great One spake, and sent Uriel to the son of Lamech

2 and said to him: Go to Noah and tell him in my name "Hide thyself!" and reveal to him the end that is approaching: that the whole earth will be destroyed, and a deluge is about to come

3 upon the whole earth, and will destroy all that is on it. And now instruct him that he may escape

The following verses and chapters talk about their judgment and confinement, then in chapter 15 Yahweh speaks to Enoch directly, who the Watchers had approached to intercede for them on their behalf…

Chapter 15

1 And He answered and said to me, and I heard His voice: Fear not, Enoch, thou righteous

2 man and scribe of righteousness: approach hither and hear my voice. And go, say to the Watchers of heaven, who have sent thee to intercede for them: "You should intercede" for men, and not men for you: Wherefore have ye left the high, holy, and eternal heaven, and lain with women, and defiled yourselves with the daughters of men and taken to yourselves wives, and done like the children

3 of earth, and begotten giants (as your) sons? And though ye were holy, spiritual, living the eternal life, you have defiled yourselves with the blood of women, and have begotten (children) with the blood of flesh, and, as the children of men, have lusted after flesh and blood as those also do who die

4   and perish. Therefore have I given them wives also that they might impregnate them, and beget

5   children by them, that thus nothing might be wanting to them on earth. But you were formerly

6   spiritual, living the eternal life, and immortal for all generations of the world. And therefore I have not appointed wives for you; for as for the spiritual ones of the heaven, in heaven is their dwelling.

Demons…

7   And now, the giants, who are produced from the spirits and flesh, shall be called evil spirits upon

8   the earth, and on the earth shall be their dwelling. Evil spirits have proceeded from their bodies; because they are born from men and from the holy Watchers is their beginning and primal origin;

9   they shall be evil spirits on earth, and evil spirits shall they be called. [As for the spirits of heaven, in heaven shall be their dwelling, but as for the spirits of the earth which were born upon the earth, on the earth shall be their dwelling.]

10 And the spirits of the giants afflict, oppress, destroy, attack, do battle, and work destruction on the earth, and cause trouble: they take no food, but nevertheless

11 hunger and thirst, and cause offences. And these spirits shall rise up against the children of men and against the women, because they have proceeded from them.

These are the demons we deal with, that most confuse as aliens. The demons roam the earth and torment mankind, causing them to sin and everything else.

These passages describe the first Watchers rebellion against the Lord. They came to earth, impregnated human women, and produced giant offspring. God then destroyed the world with a Flood to get rid of them. But it did not stop the rebellions. Genesis 6:4 states that even after the flood some of the Watchers continued to rebel against God and come to earth. At the time Israel left Egypt, they had to conquer some 20 cities of the Watchers giant children to reclaim the land of Israel as their own. The Watchers were known as the Annunaki, or the heroes of old, men of renown as mentioned in Genesis 6:4.

In Genesis, Chapter 6, from the Jewish translation of the Torah it says:

> "When men began to increase on earth and daughters were born to them, the divine beings saw how beautiful the daughters of men were and they took wives from among those that pleased them…It was then, and later too, that the Nephilim appeared on earth—when the divine beings cohabited with the daughters of men, who bore them offspring. They were the heroes of old, the men of renown."

In the Sumerian language, the term Annunaki meant "from heaven who came to earth"

Fallen Angels

The Bible is full of accounts of Israel dealing with hybrids. Genesis 6:4 says, "There were giants in the earth in those days; and also after that." They are also referred to as Rephaim, Annunaki (sons of Annuk), Emim, Zamzummim, "also after that" is referring to the Nephilim who were again found in the land of Canaan Numbers: 13:33, "And there we saw giants, the sons of Annak, which come of the giants: and we were in our own sight as grasshoppers, so we were in their sight." The word Nephilim means "violent" "causing to fall" "wonder" "prodigies" or "monsters"

When fallen angels shape-shift into a human form, they can have intercourse but not without some aberrant genetic changes. The union of these beasts with humans produced children that were different in many ways. The first apparent difference was that they developed giantism. They were giants or Nephilim. Og, the King of Bashan, had a bed that was 13 to 15 feet long; and Goliath was 6 cubits tall (9 feet). The second aberration was that they had six fingers and six toes.

The aberrant genetic defects of the Nephilim were unfortunately cloned into the DNA of mankind. These dormant genetic tendencies still surface today at times in different people; however, most of the noticeable DNA defects have been perfected over the centuries to where hybrids can easily be born into a society that never suspects them of being other than completely human. The Watchers are a guardian class of angels that were assigned to watch over the earth and protect mankind from just this sort of thing happening. The offspring giants never went out of existence; they just went "underground" to return later, which is now, during these last days.

According to the Bible, the Book of Enoch, Jubilees, Jasher, and Testimony of the Twelve Patriarchs, they rebelled against God and attempted to enslave the whole world and provoke God. According to the Book of Jasher, they not only tweaked with the D.N.A. of mankind but also with the animals. They may have produced such beasts as the Pegasus, Minotaur, the unicorn, and the dinosaurs.

In the past, scholars speculated that one day it would be hybridization which would create the antichrist and that these fallen angel-Aliens would develop and produce a creature that is fully fallen angel and fully man. A bastard angelic incarnation.

The antichrist will be Satan's seed—a Nephilim. See Genesis 3:15, Genesis 6:4, and Revelation 13. This will probably include cloning and a hybrid or of the serpent seed illuminati-bloodline.

All along, the abductions of humans breeding experiments was to perfect the ultimate breed, half man, half alien to produce Satan incarnate in man. And they have it now, and they have Mabus-Maitreya-Sananda waiting for his cue to descend to earth.

There are those who believed all the giant offspring and offspring of the fallen angels were destroyed during the flood. Not true. The Philistines were hybrids, giants i.e. Goliath. As were most of the races that Joshua and Israel had to conquer once Israel was freed from Egypt.

The Bible states that in the end times it will be just like the days of Noah. (Matthew 24:37-38, Luke 17:26) Also we believe that in Genesis 6:2 that the sons of God were fallen angels. We believe this from Job 1:6, II Peter 2:4-5, Jude 1:6 (Very important verse, "did not keep their own domain"), I Peter 3:18-20 and Revelation 9:1-12.

In the days of Noah, the fallen angels were mixing/breeding with the daughters of men (such as what the greys are doing now to humans, read about the Dulce Base). We have many hybrids in our midst, most notably the rise of "star" children who have "special" skills and talents highlighted in the movie X2 Men, released in 2003.

The mixing of genes which started with Cain's daughters, the women of Cainan, created a DNA defect called giantism. Their children were giants. Some were 30 feet tall. Demons are the spirits of the dead Nephilim (I'll just refer to Nephilim as a collective term to include all the races of the Annunaki offspring). Jedi, refers to all of the fallen angels who have ever rebelled against the Lord and were cast out of heaven. A collective term for Lucifer, his forces, and the Watchers-Annunaki.

The Bible Codes confirm that the Annunaki, had offspring called the Nephilim that were giants. The Annunaki are the Watchers. There are two different Factions within the Annunaki: the Enki and the Enlil. The draconians infiltrated and inbred within both groups of the Annunaki. The Draconians are red dragons, the same as Lucifer is.

There are groups of fallen angels competing for global dominance and control within the Third Faction of the New World Order.

These are the games they play. One group plays as good shepherds claiming to want to help mankind while they kidnap, mutilate, implant, impregnate, and use human body parts as a skin rejuvenation and coloring maintenance technique.

The other faction plays as protectors and basic non-interventionists, the good cop/bad cop strategy. We all know that when someone says they aren't in your business that that is exactly what they are into. Both of these factions seek to destroy and dominate earth, setting up the path and reign of Satan, also known as the Antichrist. Of course, they will not tell you who he really is, he will play the role of Ascended Master, Wise one, Great Teacher, Peacemaker, Messiah, a great world leader, or whatever else they can sell to a gullible population of earthlings.

There are two factions or groups within the Annunaki, known as the Enki and the Enlil.

The Enki faction of the Anunnaki

Includes but not limited to:

- Greys from Zeta Reticulum (small greys with the oversized heads who like to mutilate and experiment on humans), also includes Tall Greys (from Orion),
- Reptilians (Earth based), Lizards. These are notably in charge of establishing a one world government through our political leaders. Shape-shift into human form and also use humans as hosts to possess and work through.

- Draco-Reptilians from Orion, the ones really running the show while the others do their bidding. It is the Dracos who are the rulers over the greys and the reptilians. (There are some who believe the Nordic humanoids are Reptilians in disguise). The draco's are shape-shifters, they are the ones coming on Planet X (Rahab). The Draconians are red dragons. Lucifer himself lost his once held beauty and was turned into an ugly red dragon. The Reptilians (lizards), greys, and others are all classes of what we call aliens, but were once beautiful angels.

- Annunaki—those who joined in the Watchers rebellion against the Lord.

—and the **Enki faction of the Anunnaki, also draconian, inhabitants of Rahab,** (giant humanoids from their home planet Nibiru, a group of them stayed on earth while the others allegedly left to return sometime soon).

These are the ones who seek to harm and destroy mankind, and will do so, as they rule and dominant the earth with Satan and the New World Order.

The Enlil faction of the Anunnaki

The Enlil play a more protective role of Earth. They hate the Draconians and their ruler, Satan.

The Draconians are the archenemy of the Nordics. The Nordics hate them. They hate Satan, they hate the NWO. The coming planet X is more draconians/annunaki, shape-shifting lizards/humanoid Giants to help Satan dominate and rule the world during the tribulation period.

The Draconians are the dominant race of the (Enki), and the Nordics and other humanoid Annunaki groups are the dominant races of the (Enlil).

What gets confusing is that humanoid races joined with the Dracos, so the humanoids are in both groups.

The Annunaki and other humanoid races such as the Nordics are largely very human in appearance, approximately 7-8 feet tall, blonde hair, blue eyes (Aryans). Hitler referred to them as "the master race." Ever wonder why Hitler was so obsessed with a master race of Aryans when he was Jewish? Because he was an Edomite Jew. The Edomites were an alien hybrid line.

The Nordics and other human looking alien races were also at one time beautiful angels. Although they did not lose their good looks and forced to look like the ugly beings that Lucifer and his angels were transformed into, but they were cast out of heaven, nonetheless, and lost the qualities of being angels.

This Enlil faction includes the human looking groups, such as:

- Nordics (Lyra); Also live in an underground city underneath Mount Shasta. Human looking, tall blondes.
- Sirians (Sirius B); human looking
- Pleiedians, from the belt of Orion, human looking.
- Alpha Centaurians—human looking
- Venusians—human looking

The ancient Sumerians had their ancient culture saturated with the Annunaki. The Sumerians and the Egyptians were both Alien-hybrid races.

The Bible says Lucifer resides in the first and second heavens (space); that is where he resides, and not in hell, as many believe. Satan has dominion over the first and second heavens but not over all the alien races, only those who rebelled with him specifically and not those who rebelled later.

He rules from Orion and is a winged Draconian. He is not omniscient, or omnipresent, thus he needs his minions to cover a lot of territory on the earth to keep up with what is going on in what we call reconnaissance and spying. Are UFO's real? Yes, they have vehicles to travel in, but these are not Aliens from galaxies in other universes, but from our own solar system and own outer space.

As in the days of Noah, so shall the last days be. Although the humanoid races tend to stay out of earth affairs and tend to uphold a neutral stand and just watch everything, the Luciferian groups of aliens (greys, reptilians) will run rampant on the earth, and are doing so already. The Anuk faction working with Lucifer will arrive later to dominate so they are staying out of view for now.

We have not seen anything yet like we are going to in the near future.

They have perfected DNA manipulation and can look human while being hybrid/demon/aliens, (such as "star children" hybrids) with the ability to shape-shift into their original form and then back into a human form. No, this is not science fiction or Saturday morning cartoon central.

This is real! Fiction, Cartoons, X-Files, this was/is just conditioning to get you and your children used to seeing these things happen and to just accept it when it starts to happen more in the future.

If you want to know what is going on, sometimes the best information is in the tabloids disguised as fiction or in Hollywood movies, where they often reveal plans and agendas disguised as entertainment. One of the more notable quotes I've never forgotten was one of the last lines in a movie I watched last year from XMen 2 in which one of the hybrids says, "We've been playing by your rules long enough. Now, maybe, it's time you started to play by ours."

Phil Schneider a civil engineer contracted to build secret underground facilities for clandestine organizations (the ones dealing with these "aliens" and signing treaties with them), described the evidence he encountered that ETs would be the true rulers of a one world government, and was a reason why he and many others left the 'service' of US based clandestine organizations. Schneider was killed in what appears to be a naval assassination hit.

In fact, whenever you start to talk about or expose the government's involvement with aliens, their treaties with them or their plans, you become a target, just as Bill Cooper, former navy intelligence officer, who wrote "Behold a Pale Horse." He was gunned down in a stand off with Sheriff Deputies at his home last year.

Many have tried to wake up and warn the public about the aliens in our midst, I encourage you to read The Dulce Base book on my website at thewatcherfiles.com. It is all there. You can read all of it right from the website. Also, the Cosmic Conflict series that is on the website has great insight and information concerning what the government keeps from the public.

The Veil is being lifted, and the time will come when men will reject sound doctrine and accept doctrine of devils; (aliens) through false prophets (todays pastors). The time is coming when we will see with through the spiritual realm and those in it. We will see fallen angels masquerading as Ascended Masters, our Creators, and Beings of Light; they will deceive the world and prepare the heralding of their master…the Antichrist.

They were here before, and They will come back again.

According to the prophecy of Daniel, they will do it again in the 4th and final kingdom of the beast. "They will mingle with the seed of men." Daniel 2: 43. It is this UFO phenomena, once revealed, that could be the trigger of the falling away (apostasy) of the church as predicted in 2 Thessalonians 2:3.

The Bible warns that because the 'world' rejects the truth of the Bible that God "will send them a strong delusion, that they should believe the lie, that they may all be condemned who did not believe the truth but had pleasure in unrighteousness." 2 Thessalonians 2:11.

Chapter Six

The Prisoners of Dulce Base

There are two governments occupying the United States of America today. First, there is the traditional government established by our founding fathers, founded upon the constitution and an elected government, and there is the fascist-Bavarian-Illuminati backed "underground or shadow government" led by the Corporate-Military-Industrial government, which is fighting against traditional America on its own soil. In other words, the two sectors are the Judeo-Christian based Constitutional Republic of America and the Luciferian-cult-based Socialist empire of Bavaria, known as Bavarians or the Illuminati.

Perhaps as early as 1776, a gradual coup d'etat has been underway by Illuminati secret societies to undermine, overpower, and take over the traditional form of government in America and establish a fascist Luciferian dictatorship working under the guise of a New World Order.

Over the last 70 years since 1933, this New World Order Shadow Government funded by American tax dollars and illegal drugs and weapons trades has been developed and implemented alongside our normal government but kept hidden and out of public view by a controlled media and their trained assassins.

There is an inevitable war waiting between the elected surface government and those who will fight to defend it and the underground joint humanoid-reptilian-draconian New World Order if freedom is to be preserved. Over the past 40 years, the New World Order has successfully taken over the elections process to guarantee one of their followers is always elected as president. The American public has been deceived and played as fools by those who wish to destroy them from within. This joint alien-human domination is almost complete.

It is this joint alien-human government that has covertly undermined our elections process, lied to the American people, and have served as Presidents and many of our Congressmen since the 1970s.

Secret Societies rule our government. Not one president has been elected for the past 30 years that was not a member of the Council of Foreign Relations and Trilateral Commission run by the Illuminati. The insignia of the Trilateral Commission is the same insignia seen on Alien aircraft.

It is the fascist core of the NSA and CIA that has been the Illuminati's arm of control and protection here in America. It is this core who protect information about these bases and the alien aspect of the shadow government from being exposed. It is this core that is the direct link, not only to the aliens who direct behind the scenes, but the Vatican itself that sits at the top of it all. Not the Pope himself, but the Black Pope position, the real power in the Vatican that is hidden behind the "white" Pope and is virtually the Seat of Lucifer himself. The Draconians, dragons, of which Satan is, run the Vatican and the Illuminati and they rule this alien-human empire via Lucifer from the Vatican.

It is the NSA whose personnel reportedly pilot the black-budget UFOs between the Luna (Alternative 3) base on Mars and the Dreamland base in Area 51, Nevada. It is the NSA and DIA who operate their own UFO fleets in our skies at night, both alongside and in opposition to alien craft. The question isn't do UFOs exist, but who is flying them?

There are many secret underground facilities such as the Los Alamos base that provides an underground garage for the human-American UFO fleets located in Los Alamos, New Mexico. Even so, it is the Archuleta Mesa that is considered as the capital of the alien segment of the secret (Bavarian-Draconian-Illuminati-Alien) NWO government in America, while the Denver International Airport is the capital of the Human segment of the secret NWO government.

In many underground bases, these aliens and humans work alongside each other. However, the Lord has shown me that these humans who have agreed to work with the aliens have been taken over by them and are controlled by them. The humans have been possessed by the aliens and assimilated into the alien collective that is controlled and manipulated by Lucifer himself.

When our government officials first made contact with these aliens and started signing treaties with them, the process was under way for total Luciferian control of our government through the back door shadow government. Our government, naive to the tactics and strategies of the devil, gave him permission to indirectly work through his alien forces to work with our government and military officials, thus unknowingly allowing for the eventual possession and soul scalping of all those who would come in contact with these aliens.

Secret societies and occultic groups that have existed since the beginning of time under different names all established to worship Satan and enslave those involved to Lucifer have come into almost complete domination in these last days of almost every government in the world.

Only high ranking Freemasons, Scottish Rite, and other societies under the umbrella of Luciferian control have been allowed into positions of gaining security clearance to even come in contact with these aliens. Even at the lower ranking levels of these societies the members are required to acknowledge allegiance to Lucifer as the God of Light or God of this world or whatever other deceptive verbage they are required to recite as an oath and this is what gives Lucifer's demons and aliens permission to possess and control these humans.

The dark side and forces of evil operate on a permission basis. When someone takes an oath to Satan, no matter how deceived they are about the kind of oath they are taking, they are giving him permission to enter, demonize and possess them. Secret Societies that require oaths to join them are of the devil. Making oaths to the dark side allows the demonic to possess those in them, and when they are physically dead, Satan will possess their souls forever. In the mean time, they can be soul-scalped and replaced by aliens or demons who then take over their bodies.

This shadow government running alongside ours is controlled by these secret societies. The Council of Foreign Relations and the Trilateral Commission are, in reality, secret societies because in order to be accepted as a member in either one of them, one has to be a mason or member of one of the other Lucifer controlled societies. At this level, this allows the aliens to take complete bodily possession of the humans involved with them. And this is one of the areas where the shape-shifting phenomenon comes from.

For those involved with the shadow government and secret societies, first they lose their autonomy and individuality as human beings. Then they lose their bodies, and eventually their souls. Many have been soul-scalped and replaced by aliens themselves who now inhabit their bodies permanently.

There is evidence of an agreement called the "100 Treaty" that began in 1933 by Franklin Roosevelt between the aliens and government of the United States. It was shortly after agreements started taking place that the alien infestation of our government and elected offices started taking place. When you go to bed with the devil, you're not going to come out of it looking like an angel.

The Science Fiction movie *Close Encounters of the Third Kind* was sold to the public as the first contact we had with aliens, of course created in fiction format so no one would believe it. But in reality, contact had been made in 1933. It could have been earlier than this, but if there was contact, it's been kept well hidden.

We know there are many underground bases, practically underground cities that are kept well hidden and out of public view that sprang up as a result of having alien contact and making treaties with them.

These treaties called for joint bases to be built for the exchange of technology with aliens. Our scientists and experts would work side by side with aliens and taught the new forms of technology that had been agreed upon.

For instance, our government allows the aliens to mutilate animals and kidnap humans in exchange for antigravity technology, microchips, lasers, free energy and more. In exchange, we agreed to deny their existence, cover up their crashed UFO's, lie about human abductions and animal mutilations and keep a lid on an alien presence in this country, while these aliens mutilated animals for body parts and abducted humans for experiments, hybridization, soul scalping, chip implantation, mind control programming, dreamscape manipulation, genetic engineering experiments, crossbreeding, cloning, harvesting for body parts, using humans for food. Meanwhile our government looks the other way and protects them while they are doing it. And this still happens today.

At the same time, while the aliens have been implementing their hideous agenda onto us and worldwide, our shadow government has been taught this same technology and has been implementing it on us themselves, such as chip implantation, mind control programming, dreamscape manipulation, genetic experimenting (super soldier), cloning, and global tracking and control. We have also learned antigravity research and literally have our own UFO fleets that are built underground, tested at Area 51, painted at Area 52 and stored at Los Alamos, among other bases.

Some of the different security forces that protect and guard these bases include the Delta Force, Black Berets, Air Force Blue Berets, Secret Service, FBI Division Five, CIA Stormtroopers and the base(s) own special security themselves. It has been alleged that many involved with these security divisions have been soul-scalped or programmed to keep them under the control of the alien shadow government.

I want to focus attention here on the Dulce base. Perhaps later the Lord will lead me to expose the others. But for now this base has been brought to my attention by Him, and it would be dereliction of duty to not bring more attention to it, where it is, and what it is.

My information comes from the Most High God Himself who has given me spiritual visions about these bases, along with reports gathered and written by William Cooper, Phil Schneider, Thomas Castello, Branton, and others who risked their lives to bring information on these underground bases public. William Cooper and Phil Schneider were killed, and Thomas Castello is allegedly dead as well. Many others such as Branton, now a good friend of mine, have suffered through attempted assassinations or are constantly monitored and watched as a result of bringing public awareness to these underground bases.

The Dulce Base

This joint CIA-Human-Alien base is located under the Archuleta Mesa in Dulce, New Mexico. Close to the Colorado border and situated on the Jicarella Apache Indian Reservation, the Dulce Base is approximately 2.5 miles northwest of Dulce a town located off U.S. 64 with a population of approximately 900-1,700 people. Dulce is a small town with one motel and a gas station, but underneath the surface of the entire area lies a vast complex and network of bases and shuttle systems that criss-cross through the entire country. Dulce is the central hub.

The Dulce Base is more technically known as a Biogenetics Laboratory including but by no means limited to: Atomic Manipulation, cloning, human psychic research, advanced mind control, animal/human crossbreeding, visual and audio chip implantation, and the abduction and feeding off of humans, including children.

It is the Second largest Reptilian and Grey base in North America, yet is the Central Hub for all the underground bases. The largest base is located by Taos, New Mexico.

The Dulce Base was built on top of deep caverns that extend for hundreds of miles underground. There are 7 levels of the Dulce Base that are known of. The caverns underneath are off limits, and even most of the levels themselves are not accessible without strict security clearance to those who qualify to be on them.

The first three levels contain government offices and a garage for street maintenance. The base itself is as large as the city of Manhattan. Yes they have roads and electric vehicles to drive. The second level contains offices and a garage for trains, shuttles, tunnel-boring machines and UFO maintenance. The third level is mostly government offices.

The fourth level of the Dulce Base conducts research and experiments on the human psychy, dream manipulation, hypnosis and telepathy. All aspects of mind control programming take place here as well.

Witnesses have described huge vats containing amber liquid with human body parts on the fifth level that are constantly stirred by a robotic arm. Rows and rows, thousands of cages have also been seen holding men, women and children to be used as food and put into these vats for the aliens.

The sixth level is called "Nightmare Hall." It contains the genetic labs, and this is where the crossbreeding experiments of humans and animals are conducted. People have reportedly seen fish, seals, birds, and mice that are vastly altered from their original creations. There are multi-armed and multi-legged humans and several cages and vats of humanoid bat-like creatures up to 7 feet tall, 7 foot humans with wings and bat-like features.

On the seventh level are thousands and thousands of humans in cold storage including children.

These last few floors are the ones that the Lord has brought to my particular attention.

In their insane desire to have human bodies as their own, Aliens have perfected the ability to take a person's soul out of their body and put it 'elsewhere.' This gives them access to a human body devoid of a soul. The body is a shell, a carcass, and they can take over and possess this body and use it for themselves. This is termed as "walking-in." There are two types of walk-ins. Aliens can walk-in and possess a live human body, and/or a dead human, or in this instance, a live human who had their soul removed and then their body was taken over and walked-in by an alien.

What happens to the souls? What is a soul? A soul is what makes you-you. We are souls, and our bodies are just shells that cover our souls. Can we exist outside our bodies? Yes, as a spirit, in spirit form. The aliens are kidnapping humans and taking out their souls and then putting these souls in storage containers, even boxes, and then taking over the human bodies as their own.

The person who was abducted and kidnapped is not dead. They are still alive, but now as a soul, they are trapped in that container or storage box they were put into. They become prisoners imprisoned in these storage containers with no way out.

This is what the Lord has shown me, and this can be verified by others who have leaked out information about these bases, and if people today who work at these bases would come forward as whistleblowers, we might be able to stop this once and for all and demand a Congressional investigation (most congressmen and congresswomen don't even know these bases exist). We need to free these people and bomb these bases out of existence!

We are not ignorant now to what is going on. We know now. You are reading this and now you are one more person who knows. And it is up to us to do something about it! It's time to start screaming and not stop screaming until every last person is released as a prisoner from this base and others like it. Pray for the release of these souls. There is power in praye,r and through prayer, these souls that are being imprisoned CAN BE released and sent to the Lord or just set free from the imprisonment.

Hundreds of thousands of children and adults disappear every year in this country alone. Our government and media cover it up by under-reporting the true numbers of those who disappear, not reporting it at all, making it seem like they are just various cases of runaways, or a spouse leaving with the children. Many of these people who disappear end up in these underground bases to never be heard from again.

The Center For Missing and Exploited Children (run by the government for spin control) estimates that 300,000 children are missing each year. This number could be much, much higher and probably is. Over ten years that's 30 million children. That is a lot of food and harvested bodies for aliens don't you think? Over 30 years, that's 90 million! And our government will kill people to keep it quiet rather than keep it from happening. Why? Because in exchange for their silence, the aliens give them technology.

What technology since the 1950s has been worth over 120 million lives? Mostly children? Lasik surgery, laser beams, computers, the microchip, microwave, almost all of our advances in electronics and human chip implantation have come from the aliens. Did we need them? Many inventions by our own scientists and inventors have been confiscated by the government and then the person thrown in jail or prison to keep them from protesting.

Free energy, cures for cancers, and even Aids were found as far as 30 years ago, but the government confiscated and confiscates the inventions and patents and has killed the scientists and inventors themselves. They don't want cures when the dying industry is big business. They don't want to heal you; their purpose is to kill you. Aids was designed by them to begin with and to target and kill off undesirable populations with predisposed types of DNA. Depopulation is a big part of the Illuminati-NWO agenda. And they don't want you to have free energy when they're making billions of dollars making you pay for it. Under the New World Order, mankind serves as nothing but slaves if they're not being used as alien food. We pay for them to exist in the underground mansions we've built for them with our tax dollars. We have built them a worldwide underground super tube shuttle system. They can travel underground to almost anywhere in the world at speeds we can't even imagine on the surface earth.

Think about these things when you hear the term New World Order and/or Shadow Government.

When George Bush Sr. first publicly announced the creation of the New World Order in 1991, he was in effect publicly announcing an alien take over of our nation and the replacement of our republic and constitution with a Luciferian and Alien dominant government.

Now do you still believe the lies that he was a Christian? Who is currently our president? His son. Both are steeped into secret societies and the Bavarian Skull and Bones Society. They lied to you. The government is lying every day to us about who and what they really are.

It's time to take our country back. Our presidential election process has been ruled by the Bavarians (humans possessed and controlled by aliens) since Kennedy was assassinated for refusing to go along with them.

The Controllers of this shadow government are literally feeding off our people. They are working behind the scenes of our elected government to present to the public the lie that we still have an elected government, although they've been controlling the top offices for years through alien dominated humans. The aliens who stay behind the scenes, known as the Controllers that you don't see, are the ones directing and controlling the underground alien empire we've built for them. They are the ones directing the chip implantation of the entire nation via vaccinations, flu shots etc…and the infestation and assimilation of aliens into our society as hybrids, soul-scalped humans, and clones. And they assassinate and target people who dare expose them.

I serve the Most High God, and I am not afraid of them. May Jehovah the Most High be exalted and our nation turned back to Him so He can lead us out of the grip and hands of the Bavarians. If America chooses to ignore it, stay in sleep and do nothing, our demise is assured.

Thousands and thousands of people are being held captive in cages like animals at the Dulce Base. Even more thousands are being kept in cold storage, and even more are trapped in storage boxes with no way out.

Dulce Base is on OUR soil. It's time to bring more awareness about what this base is, where it is, and get something done about this huge network of alien underground bases. They must be destroyed!

We are at war folks. If the humans of this country don't stand up against the evil that is dominating us, we will be annihilated by them. It's not if, but when. Aliens are taking over our country and when the veil is lifted, you will start to see them more and more. Shape-shifting will become a common site; it almost already is to those in top political circles, but not the Capital Hill revolving door politicians as much as those who are "made for life" in Congress and will never lose their seats because they're part of the Bavarians. Those elected into the White House ARE Bavarians along with their entire cabinets.

Seek the Lord as to what He would have you to do. But most importantly, pray for this nation and for the captives of Dulce Base and the others just like it to be set free.

Chapter Seven

Planet Rahab—Lucifer's Seat.
Was there another planet in our solar system that disappeared? What happened to it?

Planet Rahab, is the mysterious planet that was destroyed thousands of years ago, of which is considered by many scientists and theorists today to be the creation and cause of what is known as our asteroid belt. However, the asteroid belt could simply be the pieces of destroyed asteroids themselves. Either way, they are going to have to go back to work to figure out what exactly caused the existence of our asteroid belt around the Earth because it was not Rahab, and I am going to prove it.

The Bible speaks of an existing planet called Rahab, the home of Lucifer, one of the highest ranking cherubs in God's Kingdom. It is widely held to have been located as our fifth planet in the solar system. However, Rahab, according to what I discovered in the Bible Codes, was our sixth planet, not our fifth.

Before the creation of Adam, the civilizations of celestial angels lived and cohabitated on the terrestrial planets. Throughout scripture there is a consistent reference to the first dwelling places of some of the ancient sons (and daughters) of God. It's interesting that the Bible writers themselves never mention female angels. Perhaps "sons" was another one of those sweeping generalized terms where the male pronoun was also to include females. There is no doubt there were females created, and they were menstrual, capable of reproduction. These angels created habitations on the Earth, Mars, Rahab, and the Moon.

Ezekial 28:
3 Behold you are wiser than Daniel;
every one of the secret things

is not hidden to you…
15 You were perfect in your ways
from the day you were created,
until iniquity was found in you.
16 By the multitude of your trade
they filled your midst with violence, and you sinned.
So I cast you profaned from the height of God,
AND I DESTROYED YOU,
OH COVERING CHERUB,
FROM AMONG THE STONES OF FIRE…
18 By the host of your iniquities,
by the iniquity of your trade,
you have profaned your holy places;
thus I brought a fire from your midst;

Psalm 148
"You were the anointed cherub
that covers, and I had put you
in the holy height of God…
YOU WALKED UP AND DOWN
IN THE MIDST OF THE STONES OF FIRE…
You were perfect in your ways from the day
you were created, until iniquity was found in you"

My Bible Code research into Planet Rahab uncovered a few things about this past planet. Where else should we go for information but to God Himself and let Him lead us? The Bible is His Record Book and if uncoded correctly, can reveal His mysteries.

The Bible confirms underneath its hidden layers that Rahab was indeed Lucifer's home, his ancient seat of power. He had a mansion or dwelling place there. The planet was a bustling fortress, probably much like earth is now. The people were busy, it was a nation that had turned lukewarm against their creator. They sought to break away and liberate themselves away from their creator and have their own freedom. On this planet they were capable of reproducing. They had an economic system based on money. It was politics and economics, and it was a system Lucifer wanted to turn totalitarian or communistic with all those on the planet worshipping him as God. Lucifer wanted to rule it all, and he did until he got greedy and self-exalted. He usurped God's authority by exalting himself and wanting to be worshipped as God.

Now do you see why there is nothing new about the New World Order? God told us in His Word there is nothing new under the sun. Lucifer failed in his first attempt to run a global communistic empire that worshipped him as God. Now he is going to attempt it again, and he will have 1,260 days allotted time on earth to do it. That is three and a half years from the time he proclaims to the world that he is the long awaited promised Messiah and God. This is the great delusion. The codes refer to it as a stumbling block. Who could it be a stumbling block to? Professed believers in Jesus Christ. Why? Because they fall for it. They are wavering in their faith so much that they do not understand right away that this coming Messiah known as the Antichrist is an impersonator of the real Christ and a liar.

Under Lucifer's "I" boasting he fooled the inhabitants of Planet Rahab into believing they could be completely liberated from their creator God if they worshipped him as God instead. In order for liberation, there has to be something to be liberated from. The celestial beings of Planet Rahab were under the Lord God's regulations, and they decided they had had enough of that and wanted to be free from His constraints. So Lucifer tried to cheat the real God through sedition. He became a traitor, and for this, the entire lukewarm planet was judged.

> How art thou fallen from heaven, O Lucifer, son of the morning! how art thou cut down to the ground, which didst weaken the nations!
>
> For thou hast said in thine heart, I will ascend into heaven, I will exalt my throne above the stars of God: I will sit also upon the mount of the congregation, in the sides of the north.
>
> I will ascend above the heights of the clouds; I will be like the most High"
>
> Yet thou shalt be brought to hell, to the sides of the pit. They that see thee shall narrowly look upon thee, and consider thee, saying, Is this the man that made the earth to tremble, that did shake the kingdoms; That made the world as a wilderness, and destroyed

the cities thereof; that opened not the house of his prisoners? Isaiah 14:12-17.

Most people read this as a future reference point when Satan will shake the kingdoms of the world and turn it into a wilderness. Although he will do it in the future, most overlook that he already did it in the past as well. His rebellion against the Kingship of Yahweh destroyed the nations and civilizations of several planets including the earth at that time.

When Satan and his angels rebelled, God destroyed their literal dwelling places. According to scripture, this destruction was swift and decisive with hailstones of fire. The sixth terrestrial planet which God calls "Rahab" (boaster, pride), was obliterated.

Job 26:11-13:

The pillars of heaven are stunned at His rebuke.

He quiets The sea with his power,

—and by his understanding

He shatters Rahab,

—by His spirit the heavens were beautiful;

His hand forbids the fugitive snake

Psalm 89:10 :

You have broken Rahab

in pieces, as one slain:

you have scattered your enemies

with your mighty arm.

Based on the information I obtained from the codes, God saw this rebellion, and as a result, He revoked their celestial status and annulled Himself from them. They were changed from celestial beings to terrestrial beings. Shocking the inhabitants, He then destroyed the planet with a flood of flammable hailstones with a vengeance, turning it into a wasteland, the same way He destroyed Sodom and Gomorrah. The planet was also knocked off of its axis by the pounding hailstones and sent orbiting out of our alignment of planets and into space on its own.

Lucifer was allowed to escape to the earth with some of his forces. However, many of them were confined to the planet seeking shelter in its hollow cavity and have been imprisoned in it ever since.

And this is the planet that is returning to our solar system. Planet X, or otherwise called Planet Nibiru, is the ancient Planet Rahab! The fallen angels within its cavity are reinforcement forces for Lucifer when he arrives to power on Earth as the Antichrist and becomes the global world ruler. His forces will help him run, control, and dominate earth.

I had done codes in the past on Planet X and Planet Nibiru. I just simply never made the connection to Rahab until the Lord Himself led me to it on January 17, 2004.

At the time Rahab was destroyed, other Angelic civilizations were destroyed as well that had been in conspiracy with Lucifer to overthrow God's reign. These included Mars and Earth, and perhaps others.

God brought a fire of hailstones upon Satan's midst, in the center of his greatest planetary kingdom. The planet Rahab was itself knocked off its axis and cast out of alignment in our solar system. Hailstones also impacted on the surface of mars rocking the planet causing its oceans to spill over and wash over its dry land. The Martian atmosphere was blasted into space.

On earth virtually the same catastrophes took place, hailstones of fire pounded the surface destroying the cities that had been created by the angels. Long before Adam and Eve even existed or were created.

> Jeremiah 4:23-2:
> I looked on the earth, and
> beheld it formless (laid waste) and void;
> and to the heavens, and they had no light.
> I looked on the mountains,
> and, behold, they quaked.
> And all the hills were shaken.
> I beheld and lo, **there was no man**;
> and all the cover of the skies had fled.
> I looked, and, behold, **the fruitful place**
> **was a wilderness; and all its cities**

were broken down before the face of Jehovah,
before his glowing anger. For so Jehovah has said.
The whole land shall be a desolation;
yet I will not make a full end.

Jeremiah looked into the ages before Adam and described the destruction of the earth. There were no men, (descendents of Adam), yet there had been a fruitful creation where cities had once been and which were destroyed by God's wrath. Who dwelt in these cities? Angelic civilizations. They were the angelic host called the B'nai Elohim, that existed in a perfect state on earth before the rebellion.

The same words of Genesis 1:2 "and the earth was formless and void," are written in Jeremiah 4:26. In Genesis 1:1 it says, "In the beginning God created the heaven and the earth." In the next sentence it reads, "and the earth was without form, and void" in other words, formless and void, and it is in error in most English translations. It should read, "and the earth *became* formless and void." The Hebrew word translated "was formless" in English versions of the Bible is "*toh-h,o*" a verb which means, "to lay waste." It had once been a vibrant planet, but now it laid waste, until God re-created it again.

After Satan's kingdoms were destroyed, many of the rebellious angels were bound and held until the time of judgment, the Day of the Lord, the end of the age when God gathers rebel angels on earth to receive His wrath. Other factions of the rebel angels continued existing with the ability to travel in the atmosphere outward from earth, space, and amongst the planets "the stones of fire." These angels not only lost their homes, but they lost their angelic forms as well and were cursed to look like ugly beings and creatures. They lost their beauty.

Many people get the groups of fallen angels confused and group them all together. This is not so. The Book of Enoch, quoted by Jude the brother of Jesus, and considered an important work by the early Christian Church, details the fall of the Watchers and the creation of their offspring with humans.

Lucifer's rebellion involving 1/3 of the angels, happened before the re-creation of the earth. After the earth was re-created, a second group of angels called The Watchers rebelled against God and left their first estate (heaven) to cohabitate with the women on earth.

These Watchers were judged and some were punished by being held in Tartarus or in chains under the earth. Others were allowed to inhabit the second heavens. Watchers were falling before the flood and after the flood (Gen. 6:4).

Even to this day, Watchers can fall from heaven and lose their place. All angels are created with free will and are not forced to serve God, but if they rebel against Him, they are cast out of heaven forever.

Chapter Eight

Mars: What's Really Going On and What They Won't Tell You

The sphinx, the face, the little green men. Historians seems to always have a fascination with Mars and its possible correlations with ancient Egypt.

I had to really do some digging in the codes about ancient Mars because everything on the front is what is going on up there now and what will be happening there in the future. There is a lot of activity on Mars despite what the powers that be would have you to believe.

Mars contains military bases, captives, abductees, aliens, humans being held there against their will and more people will be joining them as those caught off guard and kidnapped via the False Rapture of the Blue Beam Project when the Antichrist, posing as the messiah, descends to earth. "UFO's" will be snatching over 100,000 people off the earth to mimmick the rapture that the modern church has been conditioned to believe will happen.

And who said government and religion are separate. It makes you think that they've been working together all along to perpetrate the biggest hoax of all time. In fact, they have. The pre-tribulation teaching and the Blue Beam Project go hand in hand in working together to make thousands of people disappear, and then the world will witness the arrival of a "Messiah."

Christians will be in a panic. I see it all the time in the codes. Many people are caught off-guard by these coming hoaxes that they think are actual and real events. Often times Scripture is misunderstood, so many people will learn too late that the doctrines they've put all their faith into were and are wrong. Many believers have egos bigger than Mt. Sinai. They do not seek the truth from the Lord Himself, yet they do not want to be told they are wrong about anything.

Most will not even hear of such a possibility even existing. If these believers knew or were prepared for what was coming they would not be described as being in terror and in a panic.

From my research in the Bible Codes, I learned that the nations on Mars had joined with those on Earth and Rahab in the rebellion against Yahweh. Mars was also judged and destroyed with hailstones and fire just as Earth and Rahab had been. Although spared from being cast out of our solar alignment, it would remain largely a wasteland and most of the inhabitants left would seek shelter underground. With their cities destroyed, they would never be rebuilt to prominence again. The life they had known and enjoyed was over. But they would seek, as Satan did, to corrupt the new creation on Earth with some of their own. They infiltrated in what is now known as Egypt, or perhaps some of their own had escaped God's wrath and Judgment on the earth for its role in the rebellion against Him. The sphinx, the face on mars, and other abnomolies yet to be explained, are all in relation to their brethren on Mars. The terms Egypt—Egyptian—Remnant—Kinsman were intersecting in the Mars Codes as indicated on my website at hiddencodes.com. Ancient Egyptians were related to Martians. They were of the same seed and heritage.

Now before you start laughing at the facts, remember the little green men are not Martians. That was created for public consumption. The little green men, also known as greys, are a created species who do the footwork for the larger lizard race, the Reptilians. In short, they are slaves of the Reptilians and are controlled by them.

Satan had ruled over Mars. Although his home planet was Rahab, Lucifer had dominion over several planets, perhaps even our entire solar system at one time. We know that the Watchers inhabit Venus now and some of the unknown or unannounced planets in our star constellations. Lucifer's specific extent of rule is unknown. And how he relates to the Watchers is relatively unknown. Did he gain dominion over them when they fell? Does he govern and rule over the heavens as he once did? Or did he just retain a portion of what he once had?

The Bible indicates that fallen angels still inhabit Mars. Also known as Jedi, they are either captives of the planet, have captives on the planet, or both. Either way, Mars is still a dwelling place for fallen celestial races, ruled by Lucifer, and is going to be a stepping stone in the implementation of the New World Order and the role they play in it. There are many, perhaps millions of them, who are not free to roam around the surface of the planet, or to fly around space and visit earth as others can. These fallen angels are held captive inside Mars, which is a hollow planet, and will be released during the end times when Satan is g mission by Yahweh to release them.

Until this time, many of those who participated in Lucifer's rebellion against the Lord have been chained in captivity. During the last days, Lucifer will finally be able to release these hordes of followers to help him gain control of Earth. They will come from Planet X—Rahab, Mars, and from inside our own planet Earth.

We really do not know too much about Mars. We know the pictures are always doctored and covered up before NASA ever releases them to the public. We know that the red atmosphere is over-emphasized and exaggerated. Former employees of NASA have claimed that the atmosphere is almost identical to earth's and that there is indeed a great cover-up when it comes to Mars. Some even claim we have military bases on Mars and that the public does not know half the truth of what is really going on up there.

I don't think we do either. From what the Bible reveals in its hidden layers, there is more going on there and somewhere it's happening between a wasteland and hidden bases where people are working, living, and even being imprisoned.

The Bible reveals, that Mars had or has pilots, and they can travel throughout the cosmos. They are dimensional. They live on the planet and they can live on the earth or under the earth. Usually most aliens prefer under the earth in underground caverns, even bases, to stay out of the public's eye and the sunlight. Most are sensitive to bright light. Their claims of interdimensional travel are lies, although Lucifer himself does have access to the throne of God to accuse the Lord's believers before Him as the Word says.

What does the New World Order have to do with Mars?

We know they have bases there. The Bible reveals it. They are so secret that they are buried under the real space program in Pine Gap, Australia and covered by Black Operations secrecy. If you are familiar with the Blue Beam Project and the fake rapture to take place shortly before they herald their Antichrist as the Messiah, then you will recognize that this is the place those people captured in the fake rapture are taken. The Bible says they will be imprisoned on a base on Mars.

Mars is also the location of Mabus. The name Mabus was made popular by the prophecies of Nostradamous who predicted a world leader would rise named Mabus. However, he stated that this Mabus was just a forerunner of the real Antichrist to come. In my research, I have found that Mabus is just another name for the False Prophet to come. He will come first and be here to assist the Antichrist, the leader, the chief, the headmaster of the New World Order. He will be heralded from Mars to the Earth in a spectacular UFO and light show known as the Blue Beam Project. Our government has spent $Billions of dollars to coordinate everything needed to help Satan come to earth as the false messiah. Satan could not do it without the help of his loyal followers, those who are bringing us the New World Order.

Even the multi-billion dollar International Space Station will be used to announce his arrival to earth via a gramophone so powerful and so loud, the entire earth will hear it. The people of earth will not know where the voice is coming from, except the general direction of heaven. They will think God is announcing the arrival of His Son to Earth, when it's really just modern technology at its worst trying to deceive every person on this planet!

Chemtrails

And what are these chemtrails being spewed all over earth? I am not talking contrails, the trail from a jetliner or airplane as it flies through the air. I am talking about the thick layers of trails being laid across the sky, usually in some form of grid patterns that linger for hours. It's these chemtrails that have been known for making people sick. There has also been an increase in certain diseases, such as fibromyglaya and others since the rapid emergence of heavy chemtrail spraying in the skies over the past ten years. Little white planes have often been seen as the spewers of these chemicals. Aerodromes have also been seen. In the codes, I discovered that the white planes were associated with the United States Navy and funded by the Oval Office. That would link the NWO agenda to chemtrails since no one in the past 30 years gets into the Oval Office that does not go along with the agenda, and not all information is even made available to the President. Much of what the NSA (National Security Agency) implements, does not even have to be approved by the President or Congress thanks to a sleight of hand in legislation that makes them unaccountable. They simply fall through the cracks of accountability, and everyone looks the other way. Anything secretly funded by the Oval Office would just go through the NSA.

So what is the purpose of the chemtrails? There are several. The aerosols being sprayed make the air more conducive for holographs. Through HAARP they can make holographs of angels and Jesus appear in the sky and people would think it was real. How good is it? Just ask all those who have fallen for the Virgin Mary charade all these years. That was just practice.

And of course the NWO agenda just wants to kill you. They call it population control. It's really known as murder. Barium, aluminum, and other contaminates and poisons that have been analyzed in the chemtrails we are breathing are breaking down the immune systems of people worldwide. Flu epidemics break out, and they blame it on something else, when it's really the air you are breathing from the chemtrails. They are nothing less than bio-attacks from the sky. Read what the Bible reveals about chemtrails at my hiddencodes.com website and who are responsible for them.

Descriptive terms associated with Chemtrails from the Bible include poison, toxicant, drug, death, venom, contamination, evaporation, entrails (intestines, digestion), asthma, sky, daily, cripple, disable, dimensional, butane, arsenic, altitude, arid, bad, severe, acute, serious, evil, wickedness, atrocious, and ill.

It's not just affecting people, but our animals and land as well. Our meat is being contaminated, and our soil is getting saturated with chemicals. How long will it be before we can no longer grow our own food? Perhaps that is why our government has been trying to artificially create fruits and vegetables, and why they came out with genetically engineered foods to begin with. They know more than they are revealing to the public. Are they all involved? Is it one huge conspiracy to kill mankind? No. Only the elite in the NWO agenda really know what is going on. The "lesser, unenlightened" people only know what they stumble upon, or what they are told, and never being told the whole truth. This includes government branches, agencies, scientists, health officials, everyone and anyone that is not a card carrying member of the Luciferian loyalist NWO.

The government is compartmentalized for a reason. The government as a body contracts out services to the different members of the body, but the arm never knows what the leg is doing and vice versa. They keep everything in pieces so no one knows what the puzzle is. But they cannot fool God. And He is revealing their hideous dark agenda and plans, their sinister plans of murder, starvation, famine, and disease that they are perpetrating upon mankind in conjunction with what the aliens on Mars are doing to us.

Much of the technology considered as "black" is alien technology given to our NWO leaders to use to help implement their Luciferian agenda, along with global control and tracking. If they cannot kill you, they will always know where you are. The GPS (Global Positioning Satellite) system is just a beginning and conditioning to get you used to the idea of being tracked. If a phone call can be traced, and then the phone, the next step is the person himself. Chips, chips, everywhere chips. And eventually, into every human will a chip be required.

Chapter Nine

Planet X, Sedna and Toutatis—Signs in the Sky— The Armies of the Antichrist

In the Bible Codes, Planet X is found in Ezekiel 41:11. The Codes reveal that Planet X is the former home of Lucifer. Planet X is just an alias for the real name, Planet Rahab.

In Isaiah 14:9 it says in regards to the Antichrist, "Hell from beneath is moved for thee to meet thee at thy coming: it stirreth up the dead for thee, even all the chief ones of the earth; it hath raised up from their thrones all the kings of the nations."

Isaiah is talking about the entrance of the Antichrist onto the world scene. Will his entrance be marked with the entrance of Planet X at around the same time? They appear to be related.

I thought it remarkable that the term Planet X would have the term Hell running straight beside it.

It is returning to Earth in these last days. Why? For thousands of years it has been carrying millions of the angels who joined in Lucifer's rebellion against God. It is a hollow planet, and it has been their home and prison. In these last days Yahweh will allow their release and they will come to earth to help Lucifer gain worldwide control as the Antichrist.

The codes reveal Planet X is a habitation of evil and wickedness, a prison, a stray and errant planet that is returning to earth to rule and cohabitate with mankind. These beings are not friendly but hostile Draconians and Annunaki who will help enslave mankind, enforcing Satan's rule.

But the truth is that they do not plan on coming to share with and enlighten mankind on a better way to live, they want to destroy earth and destroy mankind! They are not planning to cohabitate with us on this planet. They fully intend to rule planet Earth.

In the codes, the Annunaki are found in Genesis 25:32 and they are found in other verses as well. I have focused on this particular code.

They are also known as Jedi or Nephilim

Who were the Annunaki? They were the Watchers, Watchmen assigned to earth to watch over Yahweh's Creation in the Garden of Eden and Earth.

It was because of them that Yahweh destroyed the world with a flood. But even after the flood, more Watchers kept revolting, and they were also punished and cast out of heaven losing their first estate and habitation. They continued to defile women and human DNA (Genesis 6:4) as the previous Watchers.

This hybridization and corruption of the human DNA is still very much a part of our world, although the giant defect has been corrected, and most hybridization goes undetected.

Why is the church silent on UFOs, Aliens, abductions, implantations, and forced breedings?

Some of the clusters I found:

> Annunaki—Assigned—Gardenland—Eden
>
> God—Creation—Watchman—Keeper—Gardenland—Eden—Mutiny—Revolt—Rebellion

also,

> Annunaki—Cherub—Angel—Seraph—Disgrace—Dishonor—Shame—Disgraceful—Mutiny—Rebellion—Revolt—Forfeit—Forfeiture—Retribution—Punishment—Yahweh—Lord—God

These Annunaki are not our creators. As you can see, they themselves were created beings by God in heaven and were assigned to watch over the earth. When they rebelled, they were cast out of heaven, their first estate, but were allowed to remain in the first and second heavens and inhabit other planets and star systems who visit the earth in UFOs.

Many of them also have underground bases here in the earth. In the following years many believe the Theory of Evolution will be discredited from the very founders themselves and their pawns. Those working the New World Order Alien Agenda will then promote through Government Disinfo Scientists that mankind was created in a test tube by these Annunaki and that these Annunaki are our creators. This is part of the grand illusion and lie at the end of days.

These Annunaki are also known as Nephilim and several other names. Instead of preaching the truth, our churches changed the truth to lies and preached the "Sons of Seth" façade, changing the truth of Scriptures. These angels were the Sons of God who rebelled against Him. Our churches also took the Book of Enoch out of the Scriptures to hide this worldwide hybridization and the truth about who these aliens are and what they are doing.

Another dominant faction of the Aliens, are the Draconians.

The term Draconian is found in Genesis 1:27 and this was funny because I stumbled on a cluster that detailed a few terms including.

> Sherry—Shriner—Troublesome—Nagger—Noisy
>
> Warfare—Combat—Dragon—Draconian

Well, I am always up for ruining a dragon party or plan.

Dragon and Draconian are relatively the same terms. Draconian means dragon. Yahweh is raising His people up to fight against them, sometimes referred to as Dragon Slayers. We do not need weapons of their warfare. We have our own.

While working on this code, the fun was just starting. It seems there is much more to come.

> Sherry—Shriner—Thrilling—Annointing—Overpowering—
> Shocking
>
> Ohio—Lineage—Provenance

I presume it's not only the orgone surprise we have waiting for them when they arrive, but the fact that I was able to decode them and expose them before they even got here. Within the same code I found:

Nibiru—Army—Residence—Home—Dragon

Carrier—Transporter—Demonic

This is more confirmation that Planet X, Nibiru, is a carrier and the home of the dragons and it is bringing them closer to earth for a showdown. They are the armies of Lucifer, the Antichrist, who will help him conquer and control the earth for 42 months. They are hostile, violent, and evil.

I've been sounding the alarms on this for years. Babylon is America, and they will conquer and control America just as revealed in the codes:

IN BABYLON (America)—Capital—Conquered

Just because they are going to conquer our country does not mean we have to lie down and make it easy for them. Fight Back! Orgone asphyxiates them. They cannot breathe where there is Orgone. Check out my websites at http://www.tearingdownstrongholds.com and http://www.orgoneblasters.com

What does orgone do? The codes reveal:

Sabotage—Disaster—Annihilation—Orgone

Toxicant—Poisonous—Asphyxia

The codes confirm that aliens cannot breathe where there is Orgone. Protect your home, neighborhood, town, city, state!!

Other terms associated with Planet X are:

Planet X—Planet—Star—Earth—Judgment—Yahweh—
End Time—Hell

This Planet will be used by Yahweh to fulfill His judgments on mankind described in the Book of Revelation:

Earth—Pole—Shake—Upturned—Old Testamer
Pentatuech—End Time

As this planet gets closer and closer to earth, it will disrupt the balance of our planet and solar system, causing cataclysmic events and a shaking of the earth, which indicates a possible pole shift.

These clusters were also found together:

> NWO (New World Order)—Babylon—Mobilization—Doorway—Opening
>
> NASA—Nuclear—Missile—Naval (does NASA try to destroy this planet)
>
> Rebel—Attack—Authority—NASA (the inhabitants of this planet will attack the authority of NASA)
>
> NASA—Bewildered—Furious—Infuriated (NASA is dumbfounded, not what they expected eh?)
>
> Cruel—Interferer—Tyrannous—Inhabitant

When will our government stop playing the games and being played as fools by the Aliens? Will it be too late before they finally see this?

The destruction and fiasco caused by the coming of this planet will begin the full mobilization of the New World Order.

Once you see this planet arrive, the arrival and entrance of the Antichrist is closely following, and we are already seeing its presence in the eastern skies in the early morning hours.

In the Book of Revelation, the Bible details horrible judgments and plagues, famines, earthquakes, wars, water contamination, and much more inflicted upon the earth after the arrival of this planet and then subsequently the Antichrist.

Hailed as a Man of Peace, the Antichrist will bring nothing but destruction and death, and this is literal, not only because of his economic policies he enforces on the world, but because by bringing in his armies to help him enforce these policies, the entrance of their planet (carrier) destroys our planet in the process.

The Aliens are coming! Sure they've been here all along, but not like they are going to be!! Millions of Anuk and Dracos helping the Antichrist take over the world! Do not be fooled, Lucifer does not need man's armies to run this world when he has got his own immortal armies! The only way to defend yourself against their evil, violent, cannibalistic 8 foot selves is with and through Yahweh!

It is the Anuk who will help enforce the mark of the beast, and it is they who will persecute and exterminate anyone who refuses to join Lucifer's one world government!

The men of old, the men of renown, will have returned, and they want to destroy you.

If you have backslidden, then get back with Yahweh. If you are on the fence, get off it.

The end days are here.

Yahweh told me, "The world has run its course; the prophecies of old will be fulfilled."

Time is ticking.

Sedna the Moon

In the Bible Codes, Sedna is found in Genesis 31:44, and it reveals that Sedna is a moon following Rahab:

Rahab—Moon—Double—Following

It's a moon of Rahab's and it's following behind it which means the "Planet" directly in front of it is Planet Rahab-Nibiru-X, the Planet NASA officially denies even exists. Although they acknowledge Sedna, they refuse to acknowledge Rahab.

Toutatis

Toutatis can be found in Genesis 41:35

NASA says it is an asteroid, another reason to never believe a word NASA says.

What does the Bible reveal about Toutatis?

Toutatis, like Sedna, is another moon-satellite-luminary of Rahab, albeit a runaway and fugitive one, but it is associated with Planet Rahab and just like Rahab, it is hollow and serves as a prison for Dracos. Currently it is just spiraling through space out of control.

Toutatis—Rahab—**Moon**—**Satellite**—**Luminary**—Fugitive—
Runaway—Courier—Hollow—Angel—Draco—Prisoner—
Mutiny—Revolt—Rebellion—Genital—Pubic—Crime—
Guilty—Imprisonment

What is really interesting about Toutatis is that it's termed a runaway, fugitive, perhaps off course, perhaps a renegade group of Draconians. Either way, its presence and arrival are threatening to the world and Babylon (USA), and the USA may nuke it and split it in half.

Will they tell the world it's a literal battle against Aliens to stop their approach to Earth? And are these Jedi purposely trying to come to earth or is this 'moon' just out of control and orbit as to where they are suppose to be and are on a collision course with Earth? Some estimate its next brush with earth to be in 2008.

Toutatis is clearly not an asteroid. The terms asteroid and comet do not even come up in this code. What is interesting is that the terms satellite and luminary seem to strike me the most as in relation to Toutatis than the term moon. Why that is, I do not know. The Hebrews grouped all three terms under the one term for moon, so it could actually be a moon or just something similar but not quite a moon itself.

Toutatis—Off-line—Divided—Runaway—Fugitive—Babylon
(USA)—Nuke—Split—Menace—Threatening—Intimidation—
Nullify—Jedi (another name for fallen angels)

One thing we do know is that many objects are coming closer to earth. Many fallen angels have been imprisoned in these moons and planets, and they will be released from their prisons in these last days to help Lucifer conquer the earth as he masquerades as the prophesied Messiah.

Some of the names for fallen angels include Aliens, Watchers, Jedi, Dracos, Draconians, Anuk, Annunaki, Reptilians, Enki, Enlil, Nephilim, Gibborim, and Locust. Some people call them demons but they are not demons. According to the Book of Enoch, demons are the spirits of the dead hybrid children of the Nephilim allowed to roam the earth. Demons are spirits and operate in the spiritual realm. Aliens have bodies, albeit usually grotesque because they lost their angelic beauty as part of their judgment. They can shapeshift—morph—transform—into human bodies and look human.

I do not think they will be worried about looking human once they arrive here in full force. Many are cloaking today to hide who and what they really are, but when the veil is lifted and Satan comes to power, they will just be as they are and who they are.

The Coming UFO Invasion, The Arrival Of The Antichrist, Satan's Seat, And Other Events Put Into Perspective

One of the things I have seen in the codes many times is the "pavilion," the Antichrist "Jesus" will rule from when he gets here. It could be a rebuilt Solomon's temple, or it could be something else altogether.

If it is the rebuilt Jewish temple, it is regarded as dishonorable and shameful because it negates and denies the real Jesus i.e., Yahushua's death on the cross and perfect sacrifice for our sins. Rebuilding this temple is a mockery of Him and what He did for us and is blasphemous. The fake Jesus who comes will approve this temple being rebuilt (obviously because it's blasphemous), but then he will overthrow and negate the treaty that allows this and sabotage and rule from it himself.

Another interesting aspect is the increase and dominance in the codes of this coming alien invasion with the Antichrist. They are his armies. And right now they are ruling behind the scenes, and guess where this Draconian seat is? The Vatican. Yes, the Draconians (dragons) are running the Vatican.

Ok not a big surprise to a lot of folks that Satan's seat is the Vatican. Satan is a dragon. And if that is where the Draconians are, then that is where Satan is. And that has also been revealed in the codes.

Keep an eye on Planet X, Rahab. As it keeps getting closer and closer to the earth, remember it is carrying the armies of the Antichrist. They are coming to earth, the veil will be lifted, and people will be able to see these aliens for what they are.

Will the Antichrist rise from the United States? He could, and it is likely and dominate in the codes that he will and I think it's one of the biggest surprises in end time events because it's something most people expect the least to happen.

The churches keep their flocks focused on Europe, or over in Israel, everywhere but here. And the codes reveal that America is the DOMINANT home of the Antichrist, unless we can prevent him from staying here because of orgone distributed all over the country and dispersed, absorbing into the atmosphere and making it impossible for the Antichrist and his armies to stay here.

There are several routes being played with different end time scenarios that are possible. These coming events are like a card game. We know the final outcome, but we can watch it unravel and the days come to a close as the events play themselves out.

The Antichrist rising from the United States is a definite card that can be played. And right now it is the most dominant card.

Most people do not think the Antichrist will come from America because the churches and prophecy gurus tell them that the Antichrist is going to be a religious leader because he masquerades as "God." Therefore, they believe it will be the pope or a religious leader rising out of the Middle East. Or some will entangle themselves with the European Union façade as the crowns on the beast of Revelation 13:1-10.

But what I am seeing over and over again in the codes is that the Antichrist is an ECONOMIC LEADER and that agrees with the same things I have found with the N.E.S.A.R.A program where I have revealed that it is the political and economic agenda of the Antichrist.

It is his political and economic platform when he comes to earth, and he will use his sidekick, fellow beast, the false prophet to enforce. It will also be what the aliens, the armies of the Antichrist will be doing: enforcing the policies of the Antichrist on mankind, showing no mercy as they do so.

The False Prophet is going to be the religious beast and cheerleader of the Antichrist. The Antichrist is going to be Economic.

The Antichrist is not proclaimed as God until he dies and comes back in a charade of UFO's, which is his demonic alien army bringing him in as God as the world looks on at this UFO invasion spectacle. But of course, it will be heralded as angels accompanying him or our ascended masters. The government will also have a hand in it with a holographic display and space station theatrics to escalate the drama of his arrival.

The churches and prophecy gurus teach that the man who is to be the Antichrist will die and then come back to life and return as God three days later. But I am finding this event of his return could be weeks, even months later, and not three days.

Chapter Ten

NESARA: The Political Agenda of the Beast

The arrival of the Antichrist is not something most of the church crowd expects to happen right now. They have been conditioned to believe in a massive disappearance around the world of believers before the tribulation period even begins. This is known as the pre-trib rapture. The Bible Codes indicate that most people are going to be completely surprised and in a panic when they see Lucifer coming through the clouds surrounded by UFOs incarnated in a human's body declaring he is the prophesied Messiah to come. Since most of the religions around the world are awaiting a messiah or prophet to come, he will be able to deceive them all because he will cater to them all.

The government has spent millions of dollars in technology, particularly on the space station to help with the theatrics of his arrival to earth. A gramophone mounted at the space station will announce his arrival and HAARP will orchestrate holographics to play along with the facade.

I helped expose government involvement from information that came out of their black operations program called the Blue Beam Project which I revealed on my website at the http://www.thewatcherfiles.com/bluebeam.htm and was later confirmed in the Bible Codes.

I learned that they will claim those in the UFOs are Ascended Masters, our forefathers and creators, or even angelic beings (his host of angels since he is God), and it will be a worldwide spectacular event, also aired live on TV as it happens.

The Bible Codes reveal massive panic among the nations of the world, not the huge acceptance he expects. Maybe that is why he is so angry when he arrives. I've never been able to pin exactly what angers him so much, but when Lucifer arrives as the Antichrist, he is angry. I do not know if he will display it or hide it, but he does not hide it for long. One of the first things he does is make a visible example of his enemies to scare everyone else into accepting him.

Imagine the panic of the millions of church pew Christians who expected to be raptured off the earth before that spectacle ever came. And instead of seeking Yahweh as to what is going on, they will head back to the same churches who have deceived them over the ages and expect to find answers.

The scary thing is, the beast's prophets are already in place. Their leading our biggest denominations and churches, and they will not give the people the truth of what is going on, but in collusion with Satan will verify that this person who came in the clouds with the UFOs is indeed the Most High God.

Those following religion have always been confident in the false belief that they will not be deceived because they are the elect. Says who? Define elect. Yes, the elect will not be deceived because they are not in the churches listening to or following man. They have sought Yahweh for the truth, and they were led out of the paganism and lies in the churches. The Lord pulled me out of them years ago. And you will hear the same thing from hundreds, even thousands of others who have sought the Lord for the truth and He has had them leave the churches as well.

Deception is not just going to be rampant then; it's everywhere now. Most people will not even know we are in the tribulation period until it hits them smack on the head, if they so choose to even wake up then.

Millions of Christians will be herded onto trains and taken to their deaths just from the acts of martial law alone, which are coming to this country. The camps are built, the trains are ready, and the churches are sleeping. When the chip or mark is enforced you have to wonder if people will recognize it for what it is. In Revelation chapter 13 it says by DECEPTION the world is deceived. I've seen in the codes how FEMA and other government organizations will enforce the beast mark as an economic policy. They are not going to tell people it is swearing allegiance to Lucifer. It's an ECONOMIC POLICY that every nation of the world puts into legislation and enforces.

The Coming Economic Policy: The Beast Prosperity Program

What is this coming economic policy that will be so widely accepted and put mankind into slavery? If that is the end result, then how does it so deceptively get accepted to begin with? Surely we are smarter than to accept something that will only ultimately lead to our own destruction.

Nothing new is going to happen in the last days. Everything happening then can be seen now working and being prepared behind the scenes.

Over the past several years, an economic policy called the National Economic Security and Reformation Act (NESARA) has come into the forefront. NESARA claims it would abolish the Federal Reserve System and provide for the buyout of all shares and facilities of the Federal Reserve Corporation by the U.S. Treasury. This NESARA would allegedly wipe out over 90% of the U.S. national debt because The Federal Reserve System's charge of fees and interest are the main causes of the U.S. national debt. Therefore, after the buyout, the government could wipe out over 90% of the debt.

NESARA sounds good at a glance. But it gets so much better. (I'm being sarcastic again). It promises to be a huge prosperity program for everyone involved.

Some of the major features of NESARA to become their propaganda battle cry is to improve liberty, prosperity, and sovereignty of average people worldwide. It is to ensure the average person's life is improved and their financial and economic assets are safeguarded.

They are ensuring liberty and sovereignty while at the same time taking it away and demanding you conform to their economic model. This is not an offer, NESARA is a demand, a global tyranny about to take over and for those who do not conform they will be subjugated and taken over by those who do.

NESARA features a new U.S. Treasury Bank system of which is imminent and claims that U.S. Bank officials have been aware of the U.S. Treasury Bank system for over a year and confirm the "Rainbow Project," that is the new U.S. Treasury currency.

The proponents of NESARA claim people in most countries will receive bank-related debt forgiveness for credit card debt, mortgages, car loans, education loans, personal loans, home refinancing mortgages, home equity loans, etc. similar to what people in the U.S. are receiving. Credit cards issued by major merchants such as Sears will also be forgiven because the funds backing these merchant credit cards are ultimately linked back to banks. And all credit unions will be forced to become a part of the new US Treasury bank system.

How can they wipe out personal debt? The plan is to pay the banks and credit unions $8,500 per credit card to erase the credit card balances and then bribe people with additional generous amounts of money to forgive the car, education, mortgage, personal, refinancing, and other loans people are held hostage by. This money is allegedly coming from funds that have been accumulating over 20 years in European banks.

According to their own publications, there will be increases in the monthly amounts of social services payments similar to what people in the U.S. receive for Social Security retirement payments, disability payments, and family support payments, etc. within a few months of NESARA being announced.

All federal government social services payments will be continued after NESARA until U.S. citizens/sovereigns/natural persons begin receiving funds from the "new prosperity" programs.

The proponents claim, the new prosperity programs will be publicly announced after NESARA is announced. Eventually, all people worldwide will have access to these programs. According to NESARA proponents, there has been enough money in the world for the last 30 years that if the money were evenly distributed, every person would be a millionaire. Five percent of the world's people control 95% of the world's wealth; NESARA frees up vast amounts of money for worldwide distribution to all the world's people except those people serving the dark agenda. NESARA initiates the distribution of vast wealth to people all across the world." You can view more of the plan in detail at http://www.omegansareliars.com/nesara-detail.htm

I think in particular, what cracked me up the most was the statement that everyone can get wealthy by worldwide distribution of money except those who serve "the dark agenda." Exactly what is considered by the beast crowd to be the dark agenda? I assume it is us, those who seek and follow the Most High God and not theirs of mammon.

The "National Economic Security And Reformation Act"—NESARA—provides major benefits to Americans including:

- Forgives credit card, mortgage, and other bank debt due to illegal banking and government activities
- Abolishes income tax
- Abolishes IRS; creates flat rate non-essential "new items only" sales tax revenue for government
- Increases benefits to senior citizens
- Returns Constitutional Law

- Establishes new Presidential and Congressional elections within 120 days after NESARA's announcement

- Monitors elections and prevents illegal election activities od special interest groups

- Creates new US Treasury currency, "rainbow currency," backed by gold, silver, and platinum precious metals

- Returns Constitutional Law to all our courts and legal matters.

- Initiates new U.S. Treasury Bank System in alignment with Constitutional Law

- Eliminates the Federal Reserve System

- Restores financial privacy

- Retrains all judges and attorneys in Constitutional Law

- Ceases all aggresive, US government military actions worldwide

- Establishes peace throughout the world

- Initiates first phase of worldwide prosperity distribution of vast wealth which has been accumulating for many decades

- Releases enormous sums of money for humanitarian purposes

- Enables the release of new technologies such as alternative energy devices excerpted from http://www.nesara.us

Also,

1. Each country MUST ABOLISH their INCOME TAXES;
2. Each country must agree to institute common law;
3. Each country must have government leaders elected by the people;
4. Each country must agree to live in PEACE;
5. Each country must bestow UNIVERSAL PROSPERITY to ALL their citizens by using the money-making formulas and processes which have a proven 200-year track record of success in providing massive prosperity

According to the Omegans, this law is already on the books, just waiting to be announced. They promote it as an act of peace, yet this is then enforced upon the entire world, regardless of whether they want it or not. It is a Global Agenda.

NESARA is nothing but a money and wealth bribe. And naturally people want to be wealthy; it's enticing. No more bills, a chance to be a millionaire, and they will buy it hook, line, and sinker.

What they do not realize is that this is the same system that actually ran interplanetary during the pre-Adamic era. There is nothing new about the New World Order. It is the old order repackaged and coming back for the last days with, once again, Lucifer at the top running it. As before, Lucifer was at the time a cherub in charge of earth and other planets, and in his greed and pride, rebelled and wanted to be like God. He boasted that he would become like the Most High. In these last days, he will be allowed to play God for 42 months. His assistant, partner, what the Bible calls the second beast, who the churches call the False Prophet, will perform miracles and claim that the Antichrist is the one who gave him the power to do it, therefore, proclaiming this "messiah" (Lucifer) the Antichrist is God.

If and When NESARA is announced, it will begin the total dissolving of the Illuminati's worldwide behind the scenes control and domination efforts. In effect, we trade one global tyrant, the Illuminati who are working to bring in their own NWO for another, the Omegans and their NESARA NWO.

The Omegans are Lucifer's armies, the Omega Army, the last days army. And they are not referring to Yahweh's armies of 144,00. The Omegans are literal aliens and those who support their agenda. As for the aliens, the Anuk, the Draco, the Reptilians and Greys. They will roam the earth and enforce the policies of the Antichrist. They are not friendly. They are hostile. When famine comes from the judgments of Yahweh for the world accepting Lucifer as its leader, the food will run out, and the Anuk, as they did before during and before Noah's time, will prey on the humans as food.

The Omegans

The Omegans are the ones behind NESARA. The leaders are Ascended Master Liar sAint Germaine (his supporters refer to him as a saint, I say he isn't, thus the spelling, sAint) and Ascended Master Liar Sananda-Maitreya. The Dove of Oneness is the official announcer for NESARA activity. The Omegans call themselves the White Knights and claim that the term "white knights" is borrowed from the Wall Street Journal and the world of big business when weaker companies are rescued from hostile takeovers by what is termed as a White Knight corporation or wealthy person. These are NOT real White Knights. From their own terminology, white knights help prevent companies from hostile takeover, yet these Omegans, with their NESARA agenda, are subtly themselves declaring a hostile takeover of the entire world!

If you do not join their program, you cannot buy or sell anything anywhere in the world. You cannot go down to the corner store and buy a loaf of bread unless you join the program, and you join this new economic program by getting the global chip that identifies you. They will promote new global technology that resembles "smart card" technology where they can put all your information on an implantable chip and without it, you cannot even continue to function in society. It will replace the need for cash; it will do everything the implantable chips you hear about now are doing; only it will be enforced instead of voluntary.

The Apostle John warned us of this in Revelation 13: 16:

> And he causeth all, both small and great, rich and poor, free and bond, to receive a mark (or chip) in (or on) their right hand, or in (or on) their foreheads:
>
> And that no man might buy or sell, save he that had the mark, or the name of the beast, or the number of his name. Here is wisdom.
>
> Let him that hath understanding count the number of the beast: for it is the number of a man; and his number is Six hundred threescore and six.

I clarified some of the terms for reasons of importance and translations. It does not matter which translation you are reading of the Bible, just know that this mark can be a barcode, a tattoo or an implantable chip, and just stay away from anything that is required to be put on or in your right hand or forehead, so you can keep functioning as a buyer and seller in society.

This is the BEAST system that the apostle warned about. When you see it, and it's already here and coming even moreso in the future to be enforced, then recognize it for what it is. It's a beast system and it's led by a beast. It is all from Satan, and it will enslave you and entrap your soul into allegiance to him. He deceived millions of angels into a rebellion against the Most High in the early ages, and he is going to use the same tactic of deception in the last days to deceive millions of people to once again join him in a rebellion against the Most High.

The Players

The two who really run the agenda for NESARA are sAint Germaine and sAint Sananda.

Some Facts About Saint Germaine:
From their own Files:

- He is known as "the man who never dies and knows everything" although he reportedly ascended only 250 years ago.

- He founded Rosicrucianism and Freemasonry in England. He did this under the name Francis Bacon (several reincarnations in every era). It was his dream to create in America a new country free of corruption, greed, and dictatorial monarchies. He was instrumental in formulating the Declaration of Independence and the constitution of the United States as they were being written by his Masonic followers who founded this nation. Their Masonic symbols can be seen on the dollar bill.

- He appears at meetings by walking through the walls

- He displays supernatural powers

- He wears a cross necklace.

Some Facts About Sananda
From their own Files:

- He is "beamed" into meetings. He just shows up in the center or somewhere in the meeting room out of nowhere. Unlike Germaine who's seen walking through the walls. (don't bang your head on the way out…)

- Ascended 2000 years ago

- He's also known as
  Maitreya http://www.sanandapromotion.com

- Is always seen with sAint Germaine

- Resembles the pictures we have grown up seeing as "Jesus." You can see their pictures at my website
  http://www.omegansareliars.com and it will not take you long

to discover that we have been led down the river of deception since we have been born and conditioned into believing what "Jesus" looks like, when it's not Him at all; it's this Sananda who is coming portraying and mocking Him. These pictures we have seen all our lives as "Jesus" are nothing more than the coming Sananda. Of course we knew those were really just artist renditions of what Jesus might look like, but to realize it was purposeful conditioning. This is going to not only put many into a panic because they are confused and think he might actually be the real Jesus, and yet anger most of those who know better. It's going to be complete chaos and confusion.

Germaine & Sananda Display Supernatural Powers

I chose not to paraphrase this but to present it all in their own terms. It's straight from the horse's mouths about their leaders.

Excerpted from http://www.white-nights911.com/Dove/edove686.htm

"Some of you have asked about the Ascended Masters; there are over 20 Ascended Masters involved, however, the two that are closely involved with NESARA are Beloved Ascended Master Saint Germaine and Ascended Master Sananda. **Beloved Ascended Master Saint Germaine ascended over 250 years ago. Ascended Master Sananda ascended over 2,000 years ago.** These two have worked together on various projects for eons and are eternal beings. The King of Swords (KOS, our White Knight in the White House) along with many other White Knights in the D.C. area frequently attends meetings where these two Ascended Masters are present in PHYSICAL form.

Beloved Ascended Master Saint Germaine is about 6'2" tall and He is "buff" as the White Knights like to say. He has dark slightly curling hair, a mustache, and a short beard. He wears a dark-violet (like the violet flame of which He often has spoken) colored tunic and pants with knee-high riding boots. Around His Neck He wears a thick golden chain with a golden cross. He has visited me on a few occasions and I have compared notes on His Appearance with others who have seen Him in physical form. I recently received an email regarding a woman who is close friends with a U.S. Senator and the Senator quoted someone in the White House who said during a meeting of the Bush cabinet, Beloved Ascended Master Saint Germaine was physically present and admonished Bush Jr. and the Bush cabinet as "school yard bullies."

I have not personally seen Ascended Master Sananda but KOS and numerous White Knights have seen Him in physical form in meetings in the D.C. area and other places.

It is impossible for anyone to impersonate the Ascended Masters (or use Their Names as aliases) because they have ways of proving who they are and have done so in World Court. Also They have unique ways of arriving at the meetings They attend. **Beloved Ascended Master Saint Germaine likes to announce His Presence by walking through a wall into the meeting room. Since humans cannot walk through walls, this is one way Beloved Ascended Master Saint Germaine conveys it is truly He who is there and His Method of arrival is a subtle reminder of His Authority. Ascended Master Sananda generally arrives at the meetings by "beaming in" like they do on Star Trek.**

The reason the Ascended Masters are here is because these are unusual times and they have planned for a long time to help Earth's people raise themselves out of the tyrannies, manipulation, and poverty in which they are now. I have frequently included articles from other sources which explain that the years between 1987 and 2012 are years about which there is both scientific and ancient cultural understandings that these years are unique. We have many indicators that we MUST change the situation on Earth for the better. The Ascended Masters have known for a long time that this "divine timing" was approaching and have been working for thousands of years on many actions which have been successful in getting us to the point that we Earth Humans are knowledgeable enough to be able to do our parts to fix the problems on our planet."

Most of the lingo common among those who are working to get NESARA announced is in itself a deceptive piece of art. Remember this is the Omegans talking, not Christians. Notice how Biblical the lingo sounds: This was excerpted from their prophecies of the coming Ascended Masters from http://www.Fourwinds10.com.

- The Father will raise up a mighty army of the faithful to deal a mighty blow to the cruel and greedy men of this world.

- He will pour out A MIGHTY GIFT upon his little ones who will CHANGE THE WORLD for the BETTERMENT of all mankind.

- He will incamp a MIGHTY ANGELIC ARMY with swords of fire TO PROTECT them.

- In those days He will call those children His Omegans.

- In Heaven's perfect timing

- Our Golden Age

They refer to the Antichrist as the Father with an Angelic Army who's coming from Heaven. It's enough to make anyone cringe, if not completely sick.

They even have their own prayer:

THE NESARA VIOLET PRAYER
Author Unknown

In the Name of the Office of the Christ, and by the power of our Mighty I AM Presence, we call upon Beloved Ascended Master Saint Germaine, and the Violet Flame, and the FORCES OF LIGHT to fully protect our White Knight Teams, and all those who are bringing NESARA to announcement, and we command and demand the continuous presence and overshadowing protection of the FORCES OF LIGHT on their behalf!

We pray that they might come to a full understanding of what it means to 'humbly ask for help' by the power of their own Mighty I AM presence, and to use THE VIOLET FIRE of Transmutation, and the gifts that the FORCES OF LIGHT, and the Galactic Federation of Worlds are presenting to the world. And so it is!—

According to their website, this prayer has been used many times over during meditations in front of the Peace Palace of the World Court, The Hague, by European Members of the NESARA Take Action Team.

When NESARA is announced as our New Economic Policy, it is expected to require over four hours of non-stop babble on television over what it is and how it will run.

According to their website, "There will be no advance public notice that the NESARA law announcement is going to be broadcast. On the day NESARA is announced, there will be an unexpected break in normal broadcasting, and the television and radio stations will announce they are interrupting regular programming to cover breaking news from Washington, D.C. As the NESARA announcement broadcast begins, we will see U.S. Supreme Court Chief Justice Rehnquist do a short introduction to NESARA; then the video tapes of Bush's and Cheney's resignation speeches will be broadcast (if it happens during their administration). Next we will see the NESARA President and Vice President Designates sworn in. The last part of the NESARA announcement will be almost four hours long and include NESARA's history, overview, and benefits.

It is long-time Omegan Al Gore who would be sworn in as the designated president. As for Vice President it would be speculation, but I will speculate on Hillary Clinton for the job since she has been a long time Omegan herself.

This is the Omegan plan. However the Bible Codes indicate Worldwide Terror and Shock! The World is NUMB! Not just at the outrageous entrance of UFO's, but the codes show this Phony-Fake-Messiah as the Announcer of NESARA is a Savage and Uncivilized Beast who murders people on live television to make an example of his enemies and those against his agenda! This entire NESARA facade will backfire, and the World is completely shocked at the whole thing!

Before the announcement, agenda plans call for a spectacular UFO invasion. The announcement will then suddenly show up on our televisions without any forewarning (similar to what they say about Matreya appearing worldwide, it's the same person). The announcement process may consist of two parts: the first part is about 15 minutes and basically includes the return to Constitutional Law, Bush's and Cheney's resignations, the swearing in of the NESARA President and Vice President Designates, and the President Designate will briefly discuss bank debt forgiveness and declare PEACE immediately. Sound familiar? The second part is a process that takes place over several days and includes speeches and lectures revealing the new policy itself of NESARA.

"They say Peace when there is no Peace"

Their Agenda is Peace and Prosperity

It all sounds good until you realize you are selling your soul to the devil to save a few bucks. It's just exchanging one global agenda for another. NESARA vs.Illuminati with Satan playing both sides.

Yes, we would all like everything NESARA promises to give, but on OUR TERMS, not THEIRS, and without mocking the depiction and resemblence of our Lord Jesus Christ, Yahushua with their Germaine and Sananda.

How many will be deceived by Sananda when they see him for themselves and realize he looks (appearance) and sounds (terminology) just like the Jesus of the Bible? Will they know this is a DECEPTION?

NESARA vs. THE BIBLE CODES

NESARA is found in Genesis 40:14 in the Bible Codes. The clusters I found within the code speak for themselves:

Ministry—Agency—Abominate—Abomination—Disgusting—Repugnant—Babylon—Omegan—Backfire

Announcement—Emergency—Brotherhood—Establishment—Undertaking—Project—Calamitous—Illusion—Delusion—Fallacy

Corrosion—Demonic—Ghoulish—Falsehood—Lie—Backfire—Babylon (USA)—Cheated—Deceived—Fooled—Nation—People

Satan—Ministry—Inform—Improve—Falsehood

Lie—Omegan

World—Numb—Shocked—Overpowering—Shocking—Announcement—Pact—Concordat—Terror—Horror—Terrorist—Phony—Lord—Yahweh—Backfire—Savage—Uncivilized—Fraudulent—Phony—Fake—Deceitful

Our real Heavenly Father is not coming in a swarm of UFOs to announce a new worldwide Economic Program. The Bible reveals quite an opposite picture of the one the Omegans are going to portray.

The Second Coming of Christ
Revelation 19:11-16

And I saw heaven opened, and behold a white horse; and He that sat upon him was called Faithful and True, and in righteousness He doth judge and make war.

His eyes were as a flame of fire, and on His head were many crowns; and He had a name written, that no man knew, but He Himself.

And He was clothed with a vesture dipped in blood: and His name is called the Word of God.

And the armies which were in heaven followed Him upon white horses, clothed in fine linen, white and clean.

And out of His mouth goeth a sharp sword, that with it He should smite the nations: and He shall rule them with a rod of iron: and He treadeth the winepress of the fierceness and wrath of Almighty God.

And He hath on His vesture and on His thigh a name written, KING OF KINGS, AND LORD OF LORDS.

In Zechariah 4:5c it says, "...and the Lord my God shall come, and all the saints with thee."

Yahushua is not coming in a UFO. He is coming riding a White Horse. He is coming with tens of thousands of His saints dressed in white robes and riding white horses, not aliens in UFOs. No announcement from a space station will be needed to get the world's attention of His arrival and descent. The world will see this HUGE PROCESSION from the skies as they slowly descend to earth, taking many hours for the whole world to witness this event. He will arrive at the Mount of Olives in Jerusalem, and by the breath of His lips He will destroy the armies gathered for the Great Battle of Armageddon.

Do not be deceived by the Imposter that is coming bearing the Name of Jesus! He is NOT the Real Jesus!

Jesus is not coming to bring peace and prosperity to the world, He is coming to judge and destroy it!

He already came as a Savior to the world, and the world rejected Him at His first coming. In His Second Coming, He is coming as a Warrior and a Judge!

The False Messiah coming will declare Peace! It is the False Prophet who will arrive first, before the Antichrist does. It is the False Prophet who arrives as "Jesus" to prepare the way for "God" the Antichrist.

Do not believe him! He will cause nothing but war, death, and destruction!

In fact, this false messiah will even come against the true believers of the real Jesus Christ, Yahushua Ha Maschiach. He will begin an earth cleansing process to kill and get rid of all those who stand in his way of implementing worldwide Satan worship unto himself, disguised as an economic program to bribe the gullible into accepting Satan's mark/chip and joining his worldwide economic system.

Do not be deceived! Do not believe his lies! The False Prophet will enforce worldwide worship of the Antichrist as God and he will cause families to go up against one another to betray those who believe in the real Son of God, even to death. Real believers in the Real Son of God will be persecuted worldwide and killed for their faith! Even by those proclaiming to be Christians!

Matthew 24:4-13

Take heed that no man deceive you.

For many shall come in my Name, saying, I am Christ; and shall deceive many.

And ye shall hear of wars and rumours of wars: see that ye be not troubled: for all thee things must come to pass, but the end if not yet.

For nation shall rise against nation, and kingdom against kingdom: and there shall be famines, and pestilences, and earthquakes, in divers (various) places.

All these are the beginning of sorrows.

Then shall they deliver you up to be afflicted, and shall kill you: and ye shall be hated of all nations for my names's sake.

> And then shall many be offended (stumble), and shall betray one another, and shall hate on another (even those proclaiming to be Christians will be deceived and turn on their fellow brethren).
>
> And many false prophets shall rise, and shall deceive many (supernatural powers).
>
> And because iniquity shall abound, the love of many shall wax cold (Christians will start backsliding).
>
> But he that endureth unto the end, the same shall be saved.

It is this NESARA that will be the political agenda and political platform of the Antichrist. When he arrives on earth, it is probably going to be the first thing he implements as he uses it to bribe a greedy and gullible world into riches and prosperity.

What better way to get 6 billion people to get a chip implanted than dangle the promises of a million dollars over their head and the elimination of debt?

And if that does not entice you, you will not have much choice because, without getting the chip or mark, you cannot put gas in your car; you cannot cash your paycheck; you cannot buy food. You are going to find yourself hostage to either getting this chip and joining the NESARA system or just dying. The only religious exemption will be at the guillotine.

It is better to die upholding your faith in Yahweh than to serve eternity in hell. Because if you join the NESARA system, the system of Revelation 13, you will automatically give your soul to Lucifer.

This NESARA system will never last or work. The judgments from Yahweh alone will throw this world into mayhem and chaos, and all the money in the world will not be able to buy food that does not exist or save you from natural disasters you cannot control. Yahweh is going to destroy this world, and no amount of money or riches will save you from it.

Better to die a martyr than enslaved to Satan and then cast into hell for eternity for turning your back on Yahweh.

> Lucifer will deceive the world. It's not an economic program ent to Lucifer. Once you receive that chip or mark promoted as incements, he owns your soul. Do not be deceived!

Chapter Eleven

The Two Beasts of Revelation 13: The Antichrist and The False Prophet

We have been waiting for the prophesied pair of the ages to arrive. And it looks like their arrival is much closer than most even suspect.

The Bible prophesies of a time when two leaders will come to power under Satan's approval and authority to deceive the world and enslave them into worshipping Satan as God. The first beast, known as the Antichrist, will not come claiming he is Satan. He will come acting like he is God, and the second beast will declare the first one is God and force the world to worship the Antichrist as one.

The Bible reveals that in the last days two beasts would arise to power and work together to deceive and destroy mankind. The Antichrist and the False Prophet.

The fact that there are two beasts is self explanatory. In Revelation 19:20 their future imprisonments are foretold:

And the beast was taken, and with him the false prophet that wrought miracles before him, with which he deceived them that had received the mark of the beast, and them that worshipped his image. These both were cast alive into a lake of fire burning with brimstone.

But before then, they will wreak death and destruction upon the world destroying our world as we know it. Prophesied end time events are like pieces of a puzzle. And every once in a while you get a piece or two, and you hang onto them because you are not sure where they fit, and then all at once, something happens, and all the pieces start to fit in the puzzle.

Each piece becomes a revelation, a realization, a hit over the head that you've been interpreting and reading something wrong. Then it comes together like a puzzle and your knowledge and understanding of events falls into place.

There are many throughout the ages who have tried to interpret last days prophecies based on man's knowledge of events of that time or what they foresee as coming. But mostly what's been going on is everyone recycling everyone else's errors and wrongly interpreting the events of the future.

There are many antichrists and false prophets in the world. It's not just one title for one particular office. There are many who hold these titles and offices and they have existed throughout the ages just as they do in this last one. The Bible calls the last two to arise in the last days beasts, because that is exactly what they are.

And that is where I will start: Revelation 13:1-10

> And I stood upon the sand of the sea, and saw a beast rise up out of the sea, having seven heads and ten horns, and upon his horns ten crowns, and upon his heads the names of blasphemy.
>
> And the beast which I saw was like unto a leopard, and his feet were as the mouth of a bear, and his mouth as the mouth of a lion: and the dragon gave him his power, and his seat, and great authority.
>
> And I saw one of his heads as it were wounded to death; and his deadly wound was healed: and all the world wondered after the beast.
>
> And they worshipped the dragon which gave power unto the beast: and they worshipped the beast saying, "who is able to make war with him?
>
> And there was given unto him a mouth speaking great things and blasphemies; and power was given unto him to continue forty and two months.
>
> And he opened his mouth in blasphemy against God, to blaspheme his name, and his tabernacle, and them that dwell in heaven.
>
> And it was given unto him to make war with the saints, and to overcome them: and power was given him over all kindreds, and tongues, and nations.

> And all that dwell upon the earth shall worship him, whose names are not written in the book of life of the Lamb slain from the foundation of the world.
>
> If any man have an ear, let him hear.
>
> He that leadeth into captivity shall go into captivity: he that killeth with the sword must be killed with the sword. Here is the patience and the faith of the saints.

In prophetic terminology the word sea is used to symbolize nations. In verse one, he rises out of the nations with seven heads and ten horns. Seven heads in particular means seven people with the names of blasphemy. The term horn signifies power and authority and crown represents that they are kings. So he rises out of the nations with 7 leaders and 10 horns (areas) of power and authority with 10 crowns.

So lets get this straight, 7 heads with the names of blasphemy, 10 horns and upon the horns 10 crowns.

Crowns represent kingship or an award. In spiritual terms crowns are rewards. For example, in heaven believers are rewarded with crowns of righteousness, or a crown of martyrdom. In political terminology the word crown would mean the highest office, kingship, or presidency.

At first glance, there seems to be more horns and crowns than people to wear them. There are 7 leaders with 10 awards/positions and areas of power and authority.

In chapter 17, we are told what these heads and horns are. In fact most of those in Bible prophecy today do not even realize that the first beast of Revelation 13 and the beast of Revelation 17 are one and the same.

Revelation 17:3:b-18

> ...and I saw a woman sit upon a scarlet coloured beast, full of names of blasphemy, having seven heads and ten horns."
>
> And the woman was arrayed in purple and scarlet colour, and decked with gold and precious stones and pearls, having a golden cup in her hand full of abominations and filthiness of her fornication:

And upon her forehead was a name written, "MYSTERY, BABYLON THE GREAT, THE MOTHER OF HARLOTS AND ABOMINATIONS OF THE EARTH."

And I saw the woman drunken with the blood of the saints, and with the blood of the martyrs of Jesus: and when I saw her, I wondered with great admiration.

And the angel said unto me, Wherefore didst thou marvel? I will tell thee the mystery of the woman, and of the beast that carrieth her, **which hath the seven heads and ten horns.**

The beast that thou sawest was, and is not, and shall ascend out of the bottomless pit, and go into perdition: and they that dwell on the earth shall wonder, whose names were not written in the book of life from the foundation of the world, when they behold the beast that was, and is not, and yet is.

And here is the mind which hath wisdom **The seven heads are seven mountains, on which the woman sitteth. (mountains is a term that can signify governments).**

And there are seven kings: five are fallen, and one is, and the other is not yet come: and when he cometh, he must continue a short space.

And the beast that was, and is not, even he is the eighth, and is of the seven, and goeth into perdition.

And the ten horns which thou sawest are ten kings, which have received no kingdom as yet, but receive power as kings one hour with the beast (10 nation alliance).

These have one mind, and shall give their power and strength unto the beast.

These shall make war with the Lamb, and the Lamb shall overcome them: for he is Lord of lords, and King of kings: and they that with him are called, and chosen, and faithful.

And he saith unto me, the waters which thou sawest, where the whore sitteth, are peoples, and multitudes, and nations, and tongues.

And the ten horns which thou sawest upon the beast, these shall hate the whore, and shall make her desolate and naked, and shall eat her flesh, and burn with her fire.

For God hath put in their hearts to fulfill his will, and to agree and give their kingdom unto the beast, until the words of God shall be fulfilled.

And the woman which thou sawest is that great city, which reigneth over the kings of the earth.

The scarlet colored beast is no doubt religion, full of names of blasphemy. One thinks of the Vatican with all their blasphemous titles of the Pope. The USA has replaced being founded on God and the Constitution with the Talmud and the NWO. And it is the Talmudic Noahide Laws, which former President George Bush Senior declared our country was based on that will give them the authority to behead anyone who worships Jesus Christ, Yahushua the Son of God (whenever they start to enforce it). In the Talmud Jesus represents idol worship, and idolatry is punishable by beheading.

It is also the Talmud on which the Vatican is now based. It is the Vatican which controls most governments of the world. However, notice the first beast of Revelation is sitting on the second beast. The first beast is not the Vatican but as we will see, the first beast is Babylon, the USA and it sits on the Vatican.

So let's move on…

> "And the beast which I saw was like unto a leopard, and his feet were as the feet of a bear, and his mouth as the mouth of a lion: and the dragon gave him his power, and his seat, and great authority"
> verse 2

Here is an assortment of animals and animals are symbolic of people or things. We know the dragon is Satan. There are many references in the Bible referring to Satan as a dragon, and even in my area of the Alien Agenda, we know that the dragons are known as Draconians or Dracos.

This is where churches start using animal terminology to fit ideas or past kingdoms that rose to power and fell. The Prophet Daniel referred to kingdoms as different types of animals.

And this is where I saw in the Bible Codes something much different for this age.

In the Bible Codes, a leopard signifies terrorism, terrorist, or false prophet. The bear represents socialism/communism, and the lion represents God, as one of His titles being "Lion of Judah," or it can be used to describe one of His own people someone who follows Him and acts within His authority.

So in verse 2 we are seeing that a leader rises who is a terrorist with a communistic agenda and speaks as if he is God or one of God's. He has the mouth of a lion. He speaks of and for God. Naturally in terms of speaking of the beast, he is apostate. He is not really of God or speaking for God. He is apostate and false, but that is not the impression he gives the people he is ruling over. They think He is a believer, a Christian, when he is really an apostate beast and terrorist pushing a communistic agenda, but he does it masking himself as one of God's own people and acting like he is under God's authority. Hitler quoted Scripture the whole time he was in power. Beasts love to quote Scripture because it dumbs people down, and they cannot get past it to see what kind of person or leader they really are behind all the religious rhetoric.

On to verse 3…

> "And I saw one of his heads as it were wounded to death; and his deadly wound was healed: and all the world wondered after the beast."

There are different interpretations on this particular passage. The beast himself dies and comes back to life, or a nation itself gets destroyed and yet comes back to power, it is healed. In chapter 17, it tells us that the heads represent a succession of leaders.

From what I have seen in the Bible Codes, the most dominant interpretation is the one where he dies, "as it were wounded to death," meaning a fake death, and then he comes back. I have never seen a country in the codes be destroyed and then come back in a short amount of time, and we know that is impossible in such a short period of time for that to happen. In this instance, we are not dealing with a lot of time. I am not saying it cannot happen, I am just telling you what I have been shown in the codes, and I have not seen that aspect in them.

What I see in the codes is the near death of a world leader, played out as a real death with a formal funeral, when he really just suffers a near death experience because something wounds him and puts him close to death. He literally just

And in the last verse talking about the first beast, verse 10 it says:

He that leadeth into captivity shall go into captivity: he that killeth with the sword must be killed with the sword. Here is the patience and the faith of the saints.

Who is it talking about here? People in general or the beast? The beast. He made war against the saints. He had them captured, imprisoned and then killed. Or even just captured and taken immediately to be killed. And Yahweh is telling him, "You have killed by the sword and now you are going to die by the sword."

"Here is the patience and the faith of the saints." Whenever we see that in the book of Revelation or told to have patience like in chapter 14:12 or in 6:11, we know justice is around the corner or already emitted. And in verse 10, Yahweh is telling us, that the beast who led His people into captivity and killed them is now going to fall victim at the same sword he held against His people. For now, his country will burn, and he will have to flee to survive. The 10 nation alliance he was a part of has betrayed him and Babylon, the country he is from, and burns America with fire.

The first beast gets 42 months to rule. You will notice after his War on the Saints and the destruction of America, he is basically a pin prick in the background. It's now the second beast who rises up and takes over.

And if you have not recognized it by now, the first beast of Revelation 13 is the President of the United States.

The Second Beast

When the second beast comes to power, he deceives and encourages the people of the world to accept the first beast as God. He even takes over the world's economy and demands that everyone get an implantable chip for technological reasons if they want to participate in the new economy. He comes with dual authority, both religious and political. He will claim the first beast is God, and he is here to help him establish peace and prosperity and his kingdom on earth.

During this time the first beast, Antichrist, is strangely silent. There is not much mention of him being active in anything other than standing around and taking credit for giving the False Prophet his "power" to perform miracles. The False Prophet claims it is from the first beast, Antichrist that he gets his power; therefore, people should worship him as God (the Antichrist).

When the second beast arises to power and authority, the first beast will take a back seat to him. They are working together in collusion to deceive the world. As "God" the first beast will step back and allow the second beast to take over. The False Prophet thus becomes the dominant beast on the scene.

The Bible Codes suggest several candidates of whom any one of them could arise to power as the False Prophet. Benny Hinn is one of them. The other is the leader of the NESARA agenda, what they call an Ascended Master, known as Saint Sananda, or Maitreya, Maitreya could also be a moniker for Mithra.

Everything about the second beast is going to be very, very deceptive. If the Sananda candidate is chosen, he is already working behind the scenes with the governments of the world to implement the beginning of the NESARA economic and political agenda of the beast. He looks just like the pictures of Jesus we have seen. We knew, most of us, that the pictures that depict Jesus are just artist renditions of what He may have looked like, but this Sananda will take it much further and actually come looking just like the Jesus in the pictures. This will deceive many. This Sananda is not a human, but an Alien, a fallen angel that deceives the gullible into believing he is an ascended master from heaven, but he really is an alien from the abyss (space), a fallen angel already working to deceive mankind.

So let's pick up where the Apostle John begins describing him in Revelation 13:11-18:

> And I beheld another beast coming up out of the earth: and he had two horns like a lamb, and he spake as a dragon.
>
> And he exerciseth all the power of the first beast before him, and causeth the earth to worship the first beast, whose deadly wound was healed.
>
> And he doeth great wonders, so that he maketh fire come down from heaven on the earth in the sight of men.
>
> And deceiveth them that dwell on the earth by the means of those miracles which he had power to do in the sight of the beast; saying to them that dwell on the earth, that they should make an image to the beast, which had the wound by a sword, and did live.
>
> And he had power to give life unto the image of the beast, that the image of the beast should both speak, and cause that as many as would not worship the image of the beast should be killed.

> And he causeth all, both small and great, rich and poor, free and bond, to receive a mark in their right hand, or in their foreheads:
>
> And that no man might buy or sell, save he that had the mark, or the name of the beast, or the number of his name.
>
> Here is wisdom, Let him that hath understanding count the number of the beast: for it is the number of a man; and his number is Six hundred threescore and six.

In verse 11 he sees a beast coming out of the earth…

> And I beheld another beast coming up out of the earth: and he had two horns like a lamb, and he spake as a dragon.

He sees a man of Jewish/Israelite lineage rising up "out of the earth" signifies the Jewish people. They are the natives of the earth, the Israelites. So that is his lineage bloodline of some degree. I am not saying he rises out of present day Israel. Hitler himself had Jewish blood. It just details he will have Jewish/Israelite blood.

He has two horns like a lamb. Horns represent power and authority and he has two, which means he has dual authority. The phrase, "like a lamb" suggests he is religious. Only this one speaks like a dragon. He is a messenger of Satan's. He is not a real lamb of Yahweh's, he is a wolf. He does not worship Yahweh. He worships Lucifer.

Verses 12-13:

> And he exerciseth all the power of the first beast before him, and causeth the earth to worship the first beast, whose deadly wound was healed.
>
> And he doeth great wonders, so that he maketh fire come down from heaven on the earth in the sight of men.

He exercises all the power the first beast ruler has, and he takes over the global government.

And he not only takes over the global government, he takes over an enforced global religion. He has two horns, which signifies dual authority. At this point, he has control of the entire world in both religious and political areas. In essence, he rules over all and gets this authority to do so by the first beast and by Lucifer.

He deceives the world by being able to produce great miracles. He makes fire come down from the sky just as Elisha did. I cannot say what kind of fire it is, but it's good enough to where it deceives millions, perhaps billions of people into believing he is God. In fact, the Bible says he deceives those living on earth.

Verse 14:

> And deceiveth them that dwell on the earth by the means of those miracles which he had power to do in the sight of the beast; saying to them that dwell on the earth, that they should make an image to the beast, which had the wound by a sword, and did live.

He then gets the world to erect an image of the first beast. This would be some type of monument or statue.

Verse 15:

> And he had power to give life unto the image of the beast, that the image of the beast should both speak, and cause that as many as would not worship the image of the beast should be killed.

The second beast then makes this statue of the first beast look and act like it's a live, living thing. And the penalty for refusing to worship or bow down before it and pay it homage is death.

This is where the armies of the Antichrist will come in. They will help the False Prophet enforce the worship of this statue around the world.

The aliens here will become enforcers, and if they see someone not worshipping the statue at an appointed time, or however they run it and enforce it, they will have the authority to execute that person.

Verses 16-18:

> And he causeth all, both small and great, rich and poor, free and bond, to receive a mark in their right hand, or in their foreheads:
>
> And that no man might buy or sell, save he that had the mark, or the name of the beast, or the number of his name.

Here is wisdom, let him that hath understanding count the number of the beast: for it is the number of a man; and his number is Six hundred threescore and six.

It's interesting that in the Bible Codes, count is another term for calculate, or computer.

This mark is a chip, a computer chip, an implantable chip. This chip is so small, the size of a dot, that it can literally be placed in anything or on anything.

The apostle says that no person anywhere will be allowed to buy anything, or even sell anything to make money, without this mark of the beast. And the mark can be this particular mark, the chip, or the beast's name, or the number of his name which calculates to be 666. In Hebrew Gematria, letters carry a value of numbers to them. With the letters that spell the beast's name, it will add to 666.

Interestingly, the interior angle of an equilateral pyramid also equates to .66666666 or just .666 You will also find in a hexagram, the "Star of David," six equilateral triangles (three sides each) surrounding a hexagon. Six times three equals 18. Six plus six plus six equals 18. 6+6+6 equals a different way to look at "666, the mark of the Beast. The Star of David was never a national symbol of the Jews until the 1800s when the Illuminati made it one.

The codes indicate this mark could also be in the form of a crucifix or cross.

Either way you have to have 1 of the 3 requirements to be able to function in any society around the world and be able to buy things to live a normal daily life, whatever that is like at that time, or to be able to sell something to make money. You cannot run a business or even a garage sale without this mark, name, or beast number on or in your right hand or forehead.

Some will claim that it is actually "on" rather than "in" your right hand or forehead. It does not matter at this point whether it's on or in. Stay away from putting anything on or in your right hand or forehead, and you will be ok. Because if you get this in your right hand or forehead, or on your right hand or forehead, you become owned by Lucifer as one of his. When you join this enforced economy, which is really enforced by Satan himself, then you become a slave to him. He owns you from that point on, body and soul.

For those who refuse, they will be beheaded. Believers in the real and true Most High God will choose to die rather than become owned by Satan. They will understand the significance of what it really means to join this global economy and world government.

At this point in the prophetic time clock, America has been destroyed. The aliens are running rampant, and the beast and false prophet are ruling probably from Jerusalem. We know they are in Jerusalem to gather the world's armies there for Armageddon.

So how will the world be warned not to accept this mark and chip if most of the Christians have already been killed from martial law? The 144,000 of Revelation chapter 7. They will be traveling the world warning them and being witnesses of the real Most High God along with the first 144,000 group of chapter 14.

The two groups of 144,000 will work together as a team to combat the armies of the Antichrist and travel the world to preach the true Gospel of the Most High.

When you research these areas of martial law and concentration camps in America, it will shock you to find that everything is already in place. And martial law is often mentioned in the news media if more terror strikes were to happen here. They are conditioning you to be prepared for it. What they aren't telling you is that it is through this martial law that the Antichrist will commence his war on the saints. They are not going to help you. They want to kill you. And they've gathered lists on just who does belong to or profess the Most High as Lord. It is through these lists that they will use to separate the people for life or death.

If your name is on a list, you will be taken to a camp and killed. They will not tell you they are going to kill you, they will tell you they are going to relocate you out of the disaster area to another. Do not believe their lies.

Do not fall for the relocation lies and scams that are coming. If they tell you to meet at a post office to be relocated to another area or state, do not go! Hide! Run!

Once an area in the US is declared to be in martial law, it will keep going and going and going until the whole country is declared to be under martial law. Seek the Lord for wisdom and listen to Him as He guides your thoughts and/or speaks to you on what to do or where to go.

Time is running out. Be aware of the double speak you hear on television and from the news media. They are purposely conditioning the masses and lying to them.

It has always been my belief based from what I have seen in the codes that the NWO would lose in their fight to run the one world government and that

NESARA would win, however the Antichrist comes from the NWO crowd to be assimilated into the Omegan NESARA crowd. And if you read in Revelation 13 and 17, you can see it in plain view. The first beast is the President of the United States. The Second Beast is the leader of the Omegan NESARA agenda. One rules the first half of the tribulation, the other rules and becomes dominant during the second half.

Those who have ears to hear, hear!

Chapter Twelve

Tearing Down the NWO Strongholds: Orgone As A Self Defense Weapon

Chemtrails, Microwave Weapons, ELF (weapons of extremely low frequency), Psychotronics, Aliens, Demons, the attacks against mankind never stop.

When I first started looking for ways to tear down the strongholds of hell and the NWO, which is almost synonymous anymore, the Most High God led me into orgone.

What is orgone? It is a natural earth cleanser, healer, and positive energy source. In the last days, the Bible says God's people will do exploits, and I know without a doubt this is one of them.

Orgone is the name given by Wilheim Reich to this vital energy found on the earth. It is also called "Ch'i," or the "fifth element."

This energy exists, in a natural way, under many different forms. It can be neutral (OR), positive (POR), or negative (DOR).

Wilheim Reich did a lot of research on the properties and behaviors of the orgone energy in the 1950's. He died in jail, after having his laboratory and much of his work destroyed by the government because they feared the truth and knowledge of orgone energy being revealed and exposed.

Chemtrails, electro-magnetic (Haarp, cell phone towers, etc.) micro-waves, and diseases are all great examples of negative orgone "at work." Without negative orgone (DOR), these technologies of death cannot work. Without DOR, without negative energy, the new world order cannot operate!

By using devices built with orgonite, it is possible to eradicate chemtrails from our skies, disactivate the H.A.A.R.P., GWEN, "cell phone" towers and other black operation programs and, at last, re-establish a positive energy balance while healing earth.

It is also possible to repel the aliens away from this planet, destroy the so-called new world order and regain our human sovereignty over this planet.

How is this possible? Could the solution really be that simple? Well, yes! Orgonite is a rather new technology, and exactly how it works is a mystery to us. We just know it does. Orgone absorbs negative energy and transforms it into positive energy, sending it back into the atmosphere as positive energy. And it is easy to make and create.

Relatively unknown, the use of orgone is gaining recognition for its ability to fight against and dissipate chemtrails. It also stops black project tower attacks, such as ELF (extremely low frequency attacks), and I have personally noticed it will keep remote viewers, aliens, and demons away from your house or yard. I have even noticed bad thunderstorms moving in the area that wreaked havoc on other areas start to dissipate by the time they reached outlying areas I had placed orgone in.

The orgone, made correctly, even has the ability to suffocate and asphyxiate evil. Evil cannot breathe where there is orgone. I have not only seen the abrupt stop of entities coming in or near my home, but found the use of orgone in the Bible Codes as well. As I decoded orgone I learned that it is definitely a protection device in these last days, so we need to arm ourselves or get clobbered and under attack.

Sure, a believer in Yahweh can rebuke evil, but if you are tired of doing it all day and every day, you will eventually learn how to arm yourself with protection against it as He showed me. This will keep it away from you to begin with, so you do not have to constantly go into spiritual warfare against the dark side.

The orgone gets absorbed into the atmosphere and will dissipate the poisons from chemtrails and keep them away from your area. And since the Annunaki are returning to conquer the earth, it will serve as a deterrent to them as well and keep them from making your town, city, neighborhood, or home their stomping ground.

Commonly referred to as tower busters, I changed the initial design of them and found a lot more effective uses for them as a result. Since the New Age crowd is adamant on making them the wrong way and using them to attract evil, I changed the name of them to reflect that it is simply not the same product capable of producing the same effects with the way I make mine. I would suggest not only putting these orgone blasters around your yard, but around your neighborhood, town, and city as well.

If you are a patriot or Christian and you want to fight against the evil being targeted against us in these last days, and even moreso to come, then get involved now and start doing something to protect yourself, your family, your neighborhood and this country. Start kicking NWO butt! All these black projects are designed to make you sick and kill you. In the last days, chemtrails will turn deadly and more targeted to kill entire areas of populations, and when the veil is lifted and Satan is cast down to earth, (Revelation 12) his armies will come with him, and they will hunt down and target believers as they become beast enforcers of his mark, number, and name (Rev. 13:17).

Even if you do not think you will be here during that time, you can leave protected areas for others to find. Placing orgone blasters near cell and other anomalous towers will help null their effects and strength against populations. Putting them in ditches, woods, bushes, even buried just underneath the surface anywhere will help the orgone to be able to absorb into the atmosphere around that area and protect it.

What can Orgone Do?

- Eliminates toxins, poisons and radiation from the air
- Defeats chemtrails and keeps your skies clear
- Improves breathing, helps those with asthma
- Promotes natural health, keeps you from catching every flu virus under the sun
- Knocks out bad thunderstorms before they get to your area, chills out tornados headed your way
- Asphyxiates evil, aliens cannot breathe around it and it burns them!
- Keeps demonic entities out of your home and yard.
- Nullifies the affects of the strong subliminal messaging NWO towers erected everywhere
- Stops ELF attacks
- Helps you sleep better

- Stops sleep abductions

- Emits positive energy, evil cannot stand being around it!

- A defensive weapon in the last days to combat aliens and the NWO

- Stops headaches and migraines, improves overall health

- Those areas gifted with orgone suffered the least amount of damage from Hurricane Charlie

Bury these in each corner of your yard to keep ELF AND OTHER MIND CONTROL weapons away from your home, not to mention unwanted demons or aliens!

Also, gift your area by placing them on the ground in bushes, trees, brush, ditches near towers to de-activate the harmful effects of towers. You can even bury them around towers if you can get that close. As long as you can get it within 1/8 of a mile from the tower, then you will neutralize it!

Some towers may take several orgone blasters to combat them. Put them in your bedroom, on top of your monitor, and on top of your cable box. A 5oz home orgone generators is best for these places. Put one in your car, carry a mini one in your pocket. There are tons of places you can put them. Stop being a victim of the New World Order and their attempts at mind control, and destroy mankind with their disease causing poison chemtrails and high tech silent weapons.

Protect Your Home From Silent High Tech Weapon Attacks!

Today, many people are getting into the silent war against the NWO agenda. Christians are being called into the war. The Lord has given us a defense mechanism in orgonite to protect our homes, yards, neighborhoods, counties, cities, states and our country. It's one step at a time and one tower at a time.

Do your part to help us take our country back from the Satanists and NWO crowd.

Is Praying Enough?

Spiritual Warfare cannot be fought without prayer. The Lord has armed us with His weapons of warfare to fight against all the tactics and strategies of the devil.

But what happens when man attacks us? Is prayer enough then? Intimidation, harassment and persecution have always been tools of the devil to use against God's believers. And in these last days we have seen high tech weapons formed and prospering against God's believers. But does not the Bible say no weapon formed against us shall prosper?

Taken in a spiritual sense, that is exactly what it means. But in a physical sense, there are many of us daily who are suffering from ELF and other types of high tech weapon attacks. Don't you take medicine to combat flues and illnesses? Orgone is a natural healer. The Lord had been stopping these attacks for me for years until He showed me a way I could prevent them from happening to myself.

For those who have suffered the affects of ELF attacks, you know how painful it is, but the fact is that by the time you are praying for God to stop the attack, you are already in a lot of discomfort or pain. Now we can prevent them from happening to begin with! The Lord has shown me that orgone will keep these attacks from happening.

Orgone is a natural healer and there are various links on this website (http://www.tearingdownstrongholds.com) where you can read about the work Wilheim Reich did with orgone. But it is not just a natural healer. It also serves as a repellent to sickness and negative energy.

And since Satan is the king of evil and negative energy, his attacks via the spiritual and physical realms are stopped and defeated by the positive energy orgone creates.

Positive energy and negative energy may sound like new age talk until you realize Jesus spoke about the very same things every time He spoke of His people being the light of the world (positive energy) and Satan being the darkness (negative energy).

For those of you who understand the power of anointing your home and repelling demons from entering it, orgone works the same way and produces the same effect effortlessly. Of course it does not replace an anointing of your home, but it is a wise secondary tool to have. It works as a repellant to negative energy, therefore, keeping it out of your home or yard, and it will work against the negative energy spewing from towers and transform it into positive energy, thereby, nullifying the affects of these towers against you.

Protect your home from being saturated from unwanted subtle mind control messaging from the towers. Protect your home from demons or aliens walking in your yard at night, or from even getting into your house at night. Protect your home from invasive remote viewers sent to harm you or spy on you. Protect yourself from ELF, EMP and other types of attacks, all from a simple natural earth product called orgone. And once you see the power of it in your home, gift your community with it by placing it around town in obscure places, best if buried, but if not possible, throw one in a ditch where it can be naturally buried by mud and water, or place it some place obscure where it will not be found. You can protect your entire community from the harmful effects of the towers, and we are finding (those actively placing orgone in areas) that these little orgone creations are nullifying chemtrails as well.

The poisons in chemtrails are making millions of people sick every year and causing the rise of cancers and diseases among the world's populations. These chemtrails are a global problem, and no one is stopping them because they are part of the NWO agenda to depopulate the earth. Stop being a victim to all this madness, and do something about it!!

The Lord has shown us what to use to defeat the tactics of the NWO and the devil, and the Lord is raising an army, one person at a time, who will help themselves and then their communities. Many brethren are already involved. Join us and do your part in slowing down and eliminating the harmful effects of towers and chemtrails in your own area. Think of the lives you are saving from sickness, disease, mind control, and high tech weapon attacks. Get involved! Do something to help tear down the strongholds of the New World Order and the devil!

Do not let yourself become enslaved by them, and do not be foolish enough to think it will not affect you, because it already is as you drive to the store and see these towers erected everywhere.

Get involved!! Do your part to help yourself and those living in your area from being affected by these towers!

Seek the Lord, and He will guide you and tell you where to put them!!

Start Today!!

You can buy them at http://www.orgoneblasters.com or you can make your own.

How can you make your own? It is easy:

Ingredients:

Clear Quartz Crystals—1-2 inch are best so you can place one inside the coil, and I put smaller ones around it as well. The more crystals the more power. If you have smaller crystals, put 2 inside the coil and one on each side of it.

Metal Shavings—shredded aluminum and copper or shredded titanium and copper. About 2/3 aluminum or titanium to 1/3 copper. I add pennies at the top for an extra copper power boost. Using pre-1983 pennies are best. You can get creative here. You can get metal shavings from metal shops that sell them, or you can use bb's, or cut up steel and copper scrubbies from Walmart or the Dollar Store. The kind you clean pots and pans with etc…they're easy to find. Cut them up in 1/2 inch pieces.

Copper Wire—you can get small roll packs of copper wire at the hardware store. About 18 gauge or smaller. I use 18 gauge. Cut off about 6 to 8 inches and wrap it around two fingers clockwise and make it coil. Then slide it off and set it into the center of your pan or cup.

Resin—I use auto bondo fiberglass resin. It's easy to find at anywhere that sells auto parts. Even Walmart has it. You can buy a quart or a gallon. It comes with a small tube of hardner. It's easiest to mix the entire thing at one time. Then try to guess proper amounts of the resin/hardner to use. You can get 12 muffin pan OB's out of a quart. Do not mix the resin till you are ready to pour it. It dries quickly and will get lumpy and hard if you do not use it right away after putting the hardner in it. Do not mix the resin in plastic. It gets too hot and dries much faster in plastic. I use old aluminum coffee cans.

12 cup Muffin pan or 3oz. dixie cups. I prefer the muffin pan because the paper is noticeable on dixie cups when tossed into woods or wherever.

Directions:

With vegetable oil grease the pan. If you are using dixie cups, the cups will not come off even if you oil them. Preferred method is muffin pan.

To keep the resin from drying too quick just add your ingredients first. Then pour resin over the top later. I spray the pan; put all the ingredients in each muffin hole, and then pour the resin over the top of the holes all at once.

If you are using pennies for extra copper power, place one in the center of muffin hole and add some metal shavings on top of it, the coil and crystals, then a little more shaving on top of that. (If you are using a gallon at a time mixed up you might want to prepare the muffin tins first. The resin can dry and harden before you get to it otherwise. A gallon can make 36-48 OBs.

For the coil cut off about 6-8 inches of the Copper wire and wrap it around 2 fingers clockwise and slide off placing the coil in center of muffin. Place some copper shavings around the coil, and add 1-2 crystals inside the coil. Looser, wider coils give me more power than tightly wound coils.

I like to put crystals both inside and around the coil.

Fill to 1/3 of top of muffin pan with the ingredients.

Pour resin over. Let it absorb; then pour more resin over it to fill it.

Let it dry. Probably about one hour. Then take out of pan. Let them dry longer.

Make in a well ventilated area, outside or in a garage.

If you are mailing them, wrap them in foil.

Let's get the word out!!

Chapter Thirteen

The Kingdom of God

What is the kingdom of God, and how do we enter into it and stay in it? The kingdom of God and the kingdom of heaven are often interchangeable. Sometimes they refer to heaven, and sometimes they speak about earth. What exactly is a kingdom? According to Webster's Dictionary it's:

1. A political or territorial unit ruled by a sovereign.
2. The eternal spiritual sovereignty of God or Christ.
3. The realm of this sovereignty.
4. A realm or sphere in which one thing is dominant

Spiritual sovereignty of God and a realm in which one thing is dominant. A territorial unit ruled by a Sovereign. That jumps out at me. If we are part of His kingdom, that means were a part of an area that is ruled by Him and under His sovereignty, His rulership.

We are within a realm in which one thing is dominant and this realm is one of Kingship. The Lord is King, and we are those who are servants of this king. This is kingdom living, being part of a kingdom and being under a rulership. However it's voluntary, and in the Lord's kingdom, it's because it's one of love. We serve the king because we love Him, because we want to serve Him, because we have chosen to become a part of His Kingdom.

Many believe His Kingdom encompasses both the earth and heavenly realm. Does it? Yes. His kingdom is in heaven, and it encompasses those within the earth that are His. For those on Earth, it is WITHIN THEM.

ENTERING INTO THE KINGDOM OF GOD

There was a man of the Pharisees, named Nicodemus, a ruler of the Jews: He came to Jesus by night, and said unto him, Rabbi, we know that thou art a teacher come from God: for no man can do these miracles that thou doest, except God be with him. Jesus answered and said unto him, Verily, verily, I say unto thee, Except a man be born again, he cannot see the kingdom of God. Nicodemus said unto him, How can a man be born when he is old? Can he enter the second time into his mother's womb, and be born? Jesus answered, Verily, verily, I say unto thee, Except a man be born of water and of the Spirit, he cannot enter into the kingdom of God. That which is born of the flesh is flesh; and that which is born of the Spirit is spirit. Marvel not that I said unto thee, Ye must be born again." John 3:1-7.

Jesus is talking about an inner transformation from being transformed from your flesh, into His spirit. No one can enter into the kingdom of God, except by this new birth, or what is called being born again of the Spirit. So how do you make that initial entrance into His kingdom to become transformed by and into His Spirit? It's easy.

Matthew 10:32, "Whosoever therefore shall confess me before men, him will I confess also before my Father which is in heaven." Confess what? That Jesus Christ, Yahushua (His real name) is the Son of God. I John 4:15, "Whosoever shall confess that Jesus/Yahushua is the Son of God, God dwelleth in him, and he in God."

"Verily I say unto you, Whosoever shall not receive the kingdom of God as a little child, he shall not enter therein," Mark 10:15. This means we enter as a child, as someone just born, and new. We have just become born of His Spirit, and we are New in Him. We must learn step by step as He teaches and leads us, and as we progress we grow from a newbie/child to an adult, wiser in Him. We start off as a beginner and advance slowly into a progressive complete fullness of His Spirit.

Getting into the kingdom of God is simple. Believe that Jesus is the Son of God, confess and repent of your sins and ask for His forgiveness, and ask Him to fill you with His Holy Spirit. Renounce the sins of your past and turn away from them. Repentance means to turn away. You are taking off the old (former self) and putting on the new (self with His Spirit) now. You are acknowledging Jesus as your Lord and Saviour, and you are coming under His rulership and into His Kingdom.

Entering the kingdom of God is by obedience to the will of God, and the new birth is evidenced by obedience, not lip service. "Not everyone who say's to me, Lord Lord, shall enter into the kingdom of heaven, but he who does the will of my Father in heaven." "But be doers of the word, and not hearers only, deceiving your own selves," James 1:22

THE KINGDOM OF GOD IS WITHIN YOU

"For, behold, the kingdom of God is within you," Luke 17:21b. How does His kingdom become a part of You? Within You? The kingdom of God is a Spiritual realm, attained by walking in the Spirit, and producing the fruit of the Spirit, which is love, joy, peace, longsuffering, kindness, goodness, faithfulness, gentleness, and self control. These are characteristics that we obtain from walking in His Spirit. And there are others.

There are the Be-Attitudes that are results of kingdom living and walking in His Spirit, not suggestions. He says Blessed are the poor in spirit; blessed are they that mourn; blessed are the meek; blessed are they which do hunger and thirst after righteousness;, blessed are the merciful; blessed are the pure in heart; blessed are the peacemakers; blessed are they which are persecuted for righteousness's sake; blessed are those who are falsely spoken of evil against, to rejoice and be glad for our reward is in heaven. Those in His Kingdom are the salt of the earth, the light of the world. His greatest commandment is for us to show love. There is no love in discrimination. God is not a respector of persons. His kingdom is for all and open to all who will receive His Kingship.

The fruits of the Spirit, the be-attitudes, love for all, these are what His Kingdom is about. On earth, His kingdom is a spiritual kingdom. His Kingdom resides within us. When we leave earth, we will go to live in His physical Kingdom called Heaven. Kingdom living is both spiritual and physical. The spiritual and physical work together, for what is done on earth, is done in heaven. Matthew 16:19 says, "And I will give unto thee the keys of the kingdom of heaven: and whatsoever thou shalt bind on earth shall be bound in heaven: and whatsoever thou shalt loose on earth shall be loosed in heaven." They work together to produce the results of His Kingdom on earth.

Building Your Own Signature Relationship With God

On Earth, kingdom living begins with building a relationship with Him, hearing His voice, being fed and taught by Him in the Spirit as we seek Him in

Spirit and in Truth. It's a unique relationship we build with the King that is an individual and personal relationship that just you have with Him. Each person in His Kingdom has this own unique and individual relationship with Him. He knows how to relate to you because you are His child. We are children of the King. So when you build that relationship with Him, it's unique, because how He relates to you, is not going to be the same as how He relates to someone else.

Your relationship with Him becomes your own unique signature with Him. Your hand written signature is your own. It's unique to you; it identifies who you are; it's your name; it's your signature. Every person has their own hand writing. No two people write exactly the same. This is how it is with God. Your relationship becomes your own unique signature with Him.

Since you've entered His Kingdom, have you built a relationship with God? Do you seek Him daily for His voice, guidance and direction? How often do you spend quiet time just waiting to hear His voice? Do you talk to Him and then Listen for Him to talk to you? God speaks to our hearts. It's a two-way building and two-way communication relationship between you and Yahweh.

That is the way that you will be able to walk in love and the fruit of the Spirit. He wants to talk to you. He has a lot to say, and He loves just being a part of your daily life. When you take time to get to know Him, you will learn who He is and what He cares about. You do not always have to be in a silent mode of prayer to talk to the Lord. I often talk to Him when I am driving, or I will go outside and stare up at the sky, or talk to Him while I am doing dishes, practically anytime.

When you pray or talk to Him, stop talking and start listening. Listen for His voice speak to your heart and spirit. Jesus does not speak to our heads. He speaks to our hearts. He cannot speak if we are always talking, and we cannot hear Him if we are not listening. Talk and Listen, the basic components of relationship building with anyone, especially the Lord who matters most.

As you begin to hear His voice and recognize Him and start to build a unique signature relationship with Him, His heart will become your heart. You will begin to beat as one. To know His heart's desires, for the church for the lost and dying world, for the hurt, the poor, the hungry, the destitute, the drug addict, the alcoholic, the prisoner, the homeless all those with needs, He cares about all of these things, not church programs and building bigger churches, and getting them full. Listen to the heart of God. You will come to know Him and to know the love He calls us to, and you will be filled with the fullness of His Spirit. You will become more of Him as you become less of yourself, and you will not be able to get enough of Him. He will dominate who and what you are.

Do you have a perfect and complete love for Yahweh, or are you wondering how somebody else is doing it? Do you feel like you are missing out on something even though you are already a professing believer? Many give Him lip service only, and never get to know the Lord they claim they serve. Are you living righteously for Him? Righteousness means right living, living right based on how He wants us and commands us to live. To be Holy, for He Is Holy. To Walk in Love, For He is Love. To Walk in His Spirit, as His Spirit is Within Us. Your love for Him will grow and reach new heights you never expected possible as you seek Him more in a Spirit building relationship. That process is what most believers simply do not understand. They do not know what it means to go into the wilderness and be alone with Him.

WILDERNESS LIVING

What is being in the wilderness? The term wilderness here is symbolic of where He takes us after we are born again unto Him. Most people get saved and head to a church to learn about Him. Yahweh desires for us to receive guidance from His shepherds, but He also seeks for us to go into the wilderness with Him where He can reveal Himself to us and show us who He is on a personal level and teach us His truths. Being in the wilderness is an experience, not a sentence.

Wilderness living is symbolic of the children of Israel who went through the wilderness for 40 years because they refused to obey God and to love Him above all else. He proved over and over He was God, and there is no other.

Yet many of them continued to make idols to worship and worship other gods. As we put idols in front of Him and let the distractions and cares of this world keep us from Him, our material possessions like entertainment, sports, etc., become the things we place before Him, they become our idols. Many were in complete rebellion and in opposition to the living God. Many do not realize they are putting their church in front of Him, and they replace building a relationship with Him with their church.

Many let their churches teach them instead of letting Him take them to the wilderness. They allow the church to replace Him. How will you know if you are being fed truth or error from the churches if you do not know what truth is? Church should reinforce what you already know, and it allows for fellowship with other believers and be a time of sharing and praising His name. But it should never become your only part of relationship building with the Lord.

"My sheep hear my voice, and I know them, and they follow me," John 10:27. "And when he putteth forth his own sheep, he goeth before them, and the sheep follow him: for they know his voice" John 10:4. "Then said Jesus unto them again, Verily, verily, I say unto you, I am the door of the sheep" John 10:7 Jesus is the shepherd and we are His sheep. His sheep know Him. They know His voice, and they follow Him. Frustration sets in for many of those when they jump ahead of Him and then feel alone. They get frustrated because they are eager to jump and run ahead. Jesus says He is the Shepherd—not you. HE WILL LEAD YOU. Do not try to jump ahead and lead Him. He does not need your help, and when you jump ahead, your out of His will, which is what leads to personal frustration. This is part of Kingdom living.

We aren't perfect. We sin and make mistakes. Jesus says, If we confess our sins, he is faithful and just to forgive us [our] sins, and to cleanse us from all unrighteousness" I John 1:9. If you sin, confess it. Turn away from it, and keep seeking Him. There is power, healing, strength and encouragement in praying with one another as well; Jesus says, "Confess your faults one to another, and pray one for another, that ye may be healed. The effectual fervent prayer of a righteous man availeth (accounts) much," James 5:16.

Those in His Kingdom need to pray together and for one another. There is strength in prayer. There is power in prayer. There is healing in prayer. There is forgiveness and restoration in prayer. And there is peace in Him knowing that He hears our prayers. We must learn to cut out all sin out of our lives and the works of the flesh. Inevitably, it can be a painful process, depending on how we yield to and cooperate with Him.

We are to walk in a spirit filled life and not to let sin dominate us. We are not to jump ahead of the Shepherd, and we are to show love to all those around us so that they can see the love of the Father through Us. We are the salt of the earth. We are the light of the world.

Living in the wilderness is a time of preparation, a place where we go to put off the old and put on the new, to get rid of the sins in our lives and learn to seek Him in spirit and prayer. It's where He perfects us to become more like Him, often referred to as sanctification. It's where we learn to hear His voice. Some people never even go to the wilderness, some never get out of it, and some are in it for a long, long time. True believers of Yahushua will have the evidence of Yahweh's Holy Spirit within them, and they are in the wilderness being taught and strengthened by His Spirit.

Learning to love and show love to all

For this is the message that ye heard from the beginning, that we should **love** one another" I John 3:11. Love is important in the Kingdom of Yahweh. In fact, it's the greatest commandment He gave to us, to love our neighbor as ourselves. Who is your neighbor? The person living beside you, in front of you, or behind you? Your friend, your associate, people you know, people you do not know you? It's anyone! it's everyone! We are to love others more than ourselves. He is telling us that we should put others first and show love at all times.

"This is my commandment, That ye love one another, as I have loved you. Greater love hath no man than this, that a man lay down his life for his friends. Ye are my friends, if ye do whatsoever I command you" John 15:12-14. There is no greater love than laying down your life for your friends as Jesus did for us. He laid His life down for His friends. We are His friends if we do what He commands us to do. If you want to be in the kingdom of God, then you must be His friend. We are not His servants. We are His friends who serve in His Kingdom, "Henceforth I call you not servants; for the servant knoweth not what his lord (boss) doeth: but I have called you friends; for all things that I have heard of my Father I have made known unto you." John 15:15.

"Beloved let us love one another, for love is of God, and everyone who loves is born of God and knows God." I John 4:7. Love should be our top priority in learning and seeking, not prosperity, not signs and wonders, manifestations, or gifts. We should be studying the love walk and how we are to walk in love as if our Kingdom citizenship depended on it, because it does. To learn how to love, we need to study Jesus. He loved others, He forgave others, He showed mercy and grace to others. He was humble and meek, never arrogant and abrasive.

Why does citizenship depend on love? Because, if we do not learn to love, we cannot claim to know Him. "Beloved, let us love one another: for love is of God; and every one that loveth is born of God, and knoweth God. He that loveth not knoweth not God; for God is love" I John 4:7,8. He that loveth not, knoweth not God. If we love one another, God dwelleth in us, and his love is perfected in us. 1Jo 4:17 Herein is our love made perfect, that we may have boldness in the day of judgment: because as he is, so are we in this world. As He is, so are we. If you are not as He is, you are not His, just fooling yourself with lip service. We must become as He is.

Mark 12:30-31 "And thou shalt love the Lord thy God with all thy heart, and with all thy soul, and with all thy mind, and with all thy strength: this [is] the first

Can We Leave His Kingdom or Lose Our Place?

He says, "He that overcometh, the same shall be clothed in white raiment; and I will not blot out his name out of the book of life, but I will confess his name before my Father, and before his angels" Rev. 3:5. There is no license to sin. There is no 'once saved always saved' if your name can be blotted out of the Book of Life. How can we feel free to sin when He has commanded us to be Holy? "Be ye Holy For I am Holy"

If a man says, I love God, and hateth his brother, he is a liar" I John 4:20a. If you are not showing love and walking in love, God's greatest commandment, then you are a liar and not one of His. If you are not abiding by His commands and seeking Him and allowing Him to sanctify you and giving up your worldly deeds of the flesh, then you are not His. True repentance is turning away from sin and the deeds of the flesh, and seeking Him in Spirit and in Truth. It's a process, but as long as you're in the process, you are His because you are seeking Him. If you are not even trying, if you are not fervently seeking Him, how can you call yourself His? Do not be deceived. There is no room for complacency in the Kingdom of God.

Sitting on the sidelines

"He that is not with me is against me; and he that gathereth not with me scattereth (driven by impulses, fly in every direction, cut to pieces) abroad," Matthew 12:30. The word "against" is kara denoting motion or diffusion or direction from the higher to the lower. Jesus said He that he who is not with me is against me, meaning they are in motion away from Him, from the higher to the lower. There is no sitting still. You are in motion for Him, either going up toward Him or moving away from Him.

In the parable of the Ten Virgins, there were some caught unprepared and left out of the wedding feast. Notice the groom did not stop to tell them "that's ok I will wait for you to get oil for your lamps." No, he left without them! They became complacent and ended up missing out on the event they had been waiting for!

Kingdom Living is being active in good works. It is being charitable and helpful and fulfilling whatever calling He has for you. There is no time to sit and watch everyone else when you yourself will be accountable for your time spent. If you are in or out of the wilderness, He will lead you. If you are neither, and sitting on the sidelines looking in, you are in danger of being left behind for not following His orders. You are in opposition to Him. "But be doers of the word, and not hearers only, deceiving your own selves," James 1:22.

Chapter Fourteen

Tell Them The Prophesied Time Has Come

These are some of the messages Yahweh has given me over the past year. I wish I had written them all down but over time, that would probably have filled volumes. I love Him, I talk to Him daily and that is just the life of a believer who truly seeks Him and follows Him, to hear from Him daily, to learn to Hear His voice, to build that one on one relationship with Him that only you and He share, a Signature Relationship. No two signatures are alike, and neither are those who have a relationship with Yahweh. You have your own unique relationship with Him. He is all I want. He is my past, present, and future. I love Him, and I am His.

The Prophesied Time Has Come

My Child, Your heart is pure before Me. I love you child. No one seeks Me like you do. You sing Me love songs. You brighten My Spirit even moreso. Yea, you fill heaven with your beautiful songs to Me. I love you child.

I will show great and mighty things to you. Write them down. Reveal them and expose them as I tell you to My faithful child. So much is stored up for you if you could only see.

I know your struggles child, for I watch over you Myself with My own eyes. You are My chosen one. You will do great things for Me child. I love you.

Fear not man, go not the way of man. You have learned to give up all to follow Me. You have the learned the truth of the truth I have showed you over the years. You have grasped what I've taught you, and you have led others to seek and follow Me in the same way.

You are the light to those in darkness. You will lead My people out of the spiritual bondage they are in and into Me. I have set you forth for this task, to lead them out of spiritual bondage. Proclaim My Name to the Nations. Tell them I have sent you. Those with ears will hear My child. For those who hear are My children, My Bride. Lead My Bride to Me. Prepare them for My coming. You have been anointed and set forth to do this work for Me. Lead them child without fear or flaw or lack of confidence because you are My chosen one to lead them. I love you child.

Continue in Me, and I will lead you to even greater heights and glory that is unimaginable to man. Know this daughter. From the day you were born, you were appointed to do My work. From the day you were conceived, I knew you and had a plan for you child, and you are following Me faithfully and walking into those plans I have set before you.

You are a blockhouse, a fortified fortress. I have surrounded you Myself with My Protection and Glory until the appointed time.

Yea, child, walk in Me. I love walking with you daily as you seek Me. You've made Me laugh like no other. You've made Me cry but those times are past. I grieved over you when you walked away in anger and in torment, but I knew when you came back to Me, that you would be with Me forever. You made your choices, and I've made mine daughter.

Go in peace, and know My hand is on and over you. You have sought My throne. You have received My words, now go and tell them the time is near for the earth to be shaken up. Tell them the time prophesied has now come. And tell them not to fear but to find safety and comfort within Me. I love you child.

Tell them!

It Is Time…

Those not sent by Me will come against you round about. They will surround you on every side. Know this child, that I am with you. I will use you as My messenger to all who seek the truth, and they will mock you and scorn you as they did Me.

The time is coming when the true servants of Mine will be here no more, taken up to be in My glory. Yes child, the time is coming.

Arm yourself with steadfastness and truth. Be bold in Me and My ways. Do not look to the left or to the right, but in Me.

You shake the gates of hell and knock the walls down of great societies and kingdoms. Expose their plans as I reveal them to you. Reveal everything I give to you My child and let Me handle your enemies. For they are great, but I AM Greater.

Do not sorrow child for those who refuse My instruction. Leave them in My hands and continue to do what I lead you to do. I have given you a sword and great anointing. Look to Me and I will lead.

The sins of the world will be destroyed in one day. You will be with Me for eternity. Regain your strength in Me and continue on, for the time is short.

I Love You My child, and daughter of David. Stand against the Giants and do not waiver. It is time.

Vision of the Shroud...

August, 2004, as I was trying to sleep, I saw the shroud of Turin appear in my mind, twice. I did not know why, but I knew what it was, His face in the shroud.

I asked Him later what the meaning of it was, why He had showed it to me. This is what He said:

It was a warning. Things are going to happen as planned. Stay focused in Me. Remember My face. I have always been with you. I know you fear Me, FEAR ME, NOT THEM. Remember ME in your distress. Do not ever lose focus of Me. The Fear of God, of ME, is the beginning of wisdom. You have much wisdom child. It is a sign to you so that you know what is ordained is of Me.

I have shown you. I have prepared you. I have kept your hand in Mine. I will not leave you.

All of heaven is watching. Your support is innumerable here. Do not let the few that rise up against you bring you down child. Rise, RISE UP! IT IS TIME!!

Every thing you have seen, nothing will throw you. I've prepared you. Seek comfort in Me and fulfill the calling I have had for you. IT IS TIME.

Thus saith the Lord your God,

The Most High God of the Universe!

All Glory and Honor is unto ME. The rest will suffer greatly!

I was asking Yahweh what is going on with the people today who say they serve Him, but seem to be drowning further in error and apostasy while thinking they are serving Him. This is what He said to me:

A Separation is Taking Place...

These people have been given way to their own delusions. Through guile, they have been deceived, and no longer will those in guile hear FROM ME. I have given them time. Now I have separated Myself FROM THEM.

Now they are under attacks from the evil they've served. There is no defense. There is no way out but through ME and to seek ME.

I've warned My people. The dividing line is coming. It starts at My house first. Those of Me will continue in Me and not be affected. Those not of Me will suffer demise, but they are not lost. They need to COME BACK to ME and stop the deceptions that put one in captivity to Satan. They become a part of what they hate the most, but they do not see it until demise and suffering hits.

Those of Me will shine forth. Be not deceived. I am not mocked. Those who have mocked Me will be brought to their knees. Those who have come against My servants will see whom they've persecuted that they ARE of Me!

The time is coming when all will see the truth in Me and know what they have done for or against Me. Much sorrow will take place, but I will bring forth My people into a newness of life in Me.

Yea child, much separation is taking place. I come with a sword to reveal the hearts and intents of men. I am starting in My house first. Then the world will become MY JUDGMENT.

Be at peace child, I love you,

Know this that when your time comes, it IS OF ME not them, for you serve a higher purpose in ME, ordained before the time.

I love you child,

Your Father in Heaven.

Fear Not...

My child,

Fear not when they come against you. Only by My hand can they get near you. The time will come when your martyrdom will arrive. Know then I am with you, and you will know beforehand. It will not come as a surprise, but neither when you expect it.

I am in control of all things. My child you will see My face and live in My kingdom with Me forever. Your children will be fine in Me. I love you child.

The time is coming. Yea, all things are coming to an end. The days close, yet My people do not realize how close My coming is. It will overtake them like a flood. Many will not be prepared. Seek My face. When I put you forth for the world to see who you are in Me, I will shine My glory upon you and all will know that you are My child, My servant, My friend.

You see suspensory and thrilling. That is because IT WILL BE child. You will shock them all, and your death will shock many. The days will never be the same again. The world will love you and see your great sacrifice for Me and will know you have been tested, tried, and found perfect in Me.

Fearless and trusting, you will go to battle for Me, and your words will warn this dark and evil world of the brightness of my soon coming thereafter.

You are an Angel of Woe who will warn this wicked and forgetful world of things to come. Yes, you will warn them all. Be confident knowing that you are complete in Me and have done all that I ask. There are not many others as self-serving to Me that you have been child. You have stayed humble in Me, and I will raise you up.

All things are coming to an end. Know this as you look around you and see the closing begin. I love you child.

Fear not them who will seek to hurt you. I am in control. Soon child, soon it will come upon you. You will speak for Me. Be prepared and do not be surprised at the events taking place. They've been planned for a long time, and you will shine as a star in heaven for Me.

I love you child.

Your Father in Heaven.

Different Ways For His Will To Be Fulfilled…

My child, I love you. There are several ways for My will to be fulfilled. Stay in Me, and I will teach you and prepare you for all of them.

The time will come, and when it does, you will step forward as the warrior you have always been and will be, and you will fight for Me, and you will lead My people and make them aware of the evil that has befallen them.

Tell them to repent while there is still time. The end time events will come as a flood, as a great deluge overcoming the people.

They will be surprised at the immediacy and how quickly things happen. But the evil forces who control and rule the world have been planning this for thousands of years. Many people will not be ready, but they (evil forces) are, and they will implement their agenda with lightening speed and agility.

My child focus now on the warnings to give My people. Ignore the naysayers for they are ripe for My judgment. Those with eyes to see and ears to hear will see and hear Me.

Many will be tested and refined at the guillotines. That is My way to test My people, those who will not love their lives unto death or betray Me. You have been tested and tried, and you are worthy. Stand with confidence in Me, lead My people to battle to war against the forces of darkness and evil.

I have spoken.

Satan Serves the Purposes of Yahweh…

Daughter,

The mixture of My children with the serpent's seed was something I allowed to serve My own purposes. Just as I allowed Satan to defile My garden, I allowed him to defile my people.

The way to truth and righteousness is through Me. It always has been and it has not changed. My priests served the people. They did not sanctify them or make them whole. I alone can do that.

Today's priests seek to save which they cannot. They lead My people to errors and doctrines of man that cannot save them, nor do they honor or please Me.

Tell them I am the door. There is no other. Those who want Me must walk through My door to Me. There is no other way.

They worship Baal and call him their god, thinking I am the one they worship. My judgment will come on this carnal and wicked system of religion. It is not of Me. Religion profits man, worship and sacrifice profits Me. Sacrifice the cares and wants of this world for the cares and wants in Me only, and you will never be unsatisfied. I can give you your heart's desire. This world cannot fulfill you. This world is an endless form of greed and want. Never satisfying, it waxes worse and worse, evil and more evil.

Yes Mithra has hidden through the ages behind every god and he will ultimately rise again to counterfeit Me and My Word. I will reveal this to you because you seek My face. You seek Me, and I will reveal great things to you because you are humble and faithful.

I love you child. Tell them the world had run it's course. It's almost time for all the prophecies of old to be fulfilled. Many will never be ready. But stay in Me for I have many things for you to accomplish before the time. Time is short. Daily seek Me so I can use you. I have shown you many things in just a short amount of time. I will show you even more.

I love you My child. If you could only see how much you make Me smile and know how much I do love you, you would never feel or want for anything again of this world. You are almost there child. Yet you still have things of Me to do in a short time. Be faithful. Be still and hear My voice. I love you, your Father, the Most High.

When I Formed You…

When I formed you, I made you for a purpose, and I will uphold my purpose. Yea, even today, I have upheld you for the days ahead.

Be not afraid child, for many will come against you. Have not I told you this already? Be strong, and of good cheer with confidence in Me because you are my mouthpiece, a chosen one, a chosen vessel of honor unto Me.

Few have sought me with their hearts as you do. I can look upon you and you are dependable unto Me. I can use you for my purposes. Yea, even as a child when you called out my Name I knew what you would be in these last days. I separated you, set you aside for Me, and you will come forth with a sword without a sheave, for your sword will never drop, nor cease. You will go forward in My Name and Conquer My enemies. Do not look to others for confirmation. Your confirmation is Me. Do not look to others for what they have, for what they have is not of Me. Look unto Me and Me only. I am your strength.

Your grandfather had the keys of spiritual wisdom. I passed on the keys of wisdom to his children. You have regained this key of spiritual wisdom for the last days and the days you are in, and you will proclaim a sword against those who do not know Me.

I have designated and reserved you for these purposes. Stand tall and be proud of who you are and do not look down look up. Look up at Me as you do throughout the day and you sing to me and I hear you child, I know you Love Me. I know you worship Me above all else, and for this my child, I know you are My Friend.

What greater love can be given but to a friend indeed. I love you child.

I will set you above the mountains with a Sword. I will anoint this Sword, and wherever you go, you will be annointed in Me. Whatever you do is of Me. Whatever you think will be of Me. Whatever you say will be of Me, I am bringing you to a new level in Me because you have been tested and tried, and have been found faithful.

No greater testing has been given among man in these last days than what you have endured. You have stood in Me, and I so love you child. Walk with Me. Commune with Me. I love to hear you laugh. So many times I've just wanted to be right there next to you, so you could literally see me and enjoy being in my visible presence. I long for that child.

The day is coming when you will be exalted among my Servants. My Warrior, you will lead them to many battles and victories in my Name.

I want you to know that I know how much you have loved Me. Be confident. Be still child, for I have spoken.

I Am Coming For A Bride...

I am coming for a bride that is found without guile. In Me they are spotless and blameless because they walk in ME and desire daily to be in ME and get to know Me.

They do not follow Me with their lips. They follow Me with their hearts.

Many will be left behind to their own devices. They say they know Me, but they do not. They seek truth as it is in man and not as it is in Me.

Many claim My Name and do not know Me intimately. Have not I said, "My sheep hear my voice and they know Me, and they follow Me?"

I am coming for MY sheep. And these sheep will transform the world in the dark and evil days ahead when Satan takes complete rule of the earth.

Many victories will be won for Me in the dark and evil days, and My sheep will lead the way in the calling of righteousness and repentence.

My child do not fear the things that you see or hear that are coming. Stay in Me. You know there is no fear in Me. So draw close to Me, and stay there even at the darkest hours, for I am your Light.

I am coming soon for My sheep. You will hear My calling and see Me face to face. I love you child. Thus saith the Lord your God.

Conclusion

Terrorism, martial law, chemtrails, concentration camps, and it goes on and on. There are many things I did not cover in this book because of space, yet I do cover these topics on my websites.

These events will all trigger the rise of the Antichrist and the War on the Saints, which happens long before the mark of the beast is enforced upon the world.

Most people expect a mystery rapture to occur that will ensure them a one way ticket off earth when the tribulation period begins. And that simply is not true.

Yahushua the real name of Jesus said, "I am the way, the truth, and the life, no man cometh unto the Father but by Me."

If you want to get to heaven, you must seek the Father, Yahweh, the Most High God, and it is through the sacrifice of His Son, Yahushua, that we can do that.

It's time to choose whom will you follow? The True Son of God? Or the hoax that is on the way claiming he is God and demands for you to accept his mark (chip implant) on or in your right hand or forehead to show your loyalty to him (Satan)? It's time to take a stand now for Yahushua and eternal life in heaven! Our only safety is in Yahushua!

"For God so loved the world, that He sent His only begotten Son, that whosoever believeth on Him, should not perish but have everlasting life" John 3:16

If you want Victory over the evil that is pervading this world, then you need Yahushua.

If you want victory over the technology that our government and military are trying to destroy you with, then YOU NEED YAHUSHUA.

If you want eternal life in heaven, then YOU NEED YAHSHUA.

Say this prayer between you and Him.

Dear Heavenly Father,

Lord I know I am a sinner and that without you I am lost.

Please forgive me for my sins, for the sins I've committed against others, and help me to forgive those that have sinned against me.

I believe that you sent your Son, Jesus (Yahshuah), to die on the cross, that He rose again three days later, and that He is coming back for me.

I accept your gift of salvation, and ask that you, Yahushuah, come into my heart and be my Saviour. Fill me with your Holy Spirit and give me all the blessings promised in your Word and those that you want to give to me.

Help me to live for you from this day on.

Thank you Father for sending your Son. Thank you Jesus for saving me and being my personal Saviour.

In Yahushua's Name, Amen.

Now Seek HIM...with all Your MIND, SOUL and STRENGTH. You do not "try" Yahushua...you build a relationship with HIM.

Seek Him Daily. Learn who He is and about His Kingdom.

Websites Run By Sherry Shriner

http://www.sherryshriner.com

http://www.thewatcherfiles.com

http://www.hiddencodes.com

http://www.lastdaysprophecies.com

http://www.rahabisreturning.com

http://www.omegansareliars.com

http://www.warfaresaint.com

http://www.justgivemethetruth.com

http://www.tearingdownstrongholds.com

http://www.orgoneblasters.com

http://sherryshriner.blogspot.com

http://www.sherrytalkradio.com

http://www.saintsunderattack.com

Sherry can be heard every Saturday night at 8pm EST
on Reality Radio Network

http://www.realityradionetwork.com

or go to

http://www.sherrytalkradio.com

How To Make Orgone Blasters

Ingredients:

Clear Quartz Crystals—1-2 inch are best so you can place one inside the coil, and I put smaller ones around it as well. The more crystals the more power. If you have smaller crystals, put 2 inside the coil and one on each side of it.

Metal Shavings—shredded aluminum and copper or shredded titanium and copper. About 2/3 aluminum or titanium to 1/3 copper. I add pennies at the top for an extra copper power boost. Using pre-1983 pennies are best. You can get creative here. You can get metal shavings from metal shops that sell them, or you can use bb's, or cut up steel and copper scrubbies from Walmart or the Dollar Store. The kind you clean pots and pans with etc…they're easy to find. Cut them up in 1/2 inch pieces.

Copper Wire—you can get small roll packs of copper wire at the hardware store. About 18 gauge or smaller. I use 18 gauge. Cut off about 6 to 8 inches and wrap it around two fingers clockwise and make it coil. Then slide it off and set it into the center of your pan or cup.

Resin—I use auto bondo fiberglass resin. It's easy to find at anywhere that sells auto parts. Even Walmart has it. You can buy a quart or a gallon. It comes with a small tube of hardner. It's easiest to mix the entire thing at one time than it is to try to guess proper amounts of the resin/hardner to use. You can get 12 muffin pan OB's out of a quart. Do not mix the resin till you are ready to pour it. It dries quickly and will get lumpy and hard if you do not use it right away after putting the hardner in it. Do not mix the resin in plastic. It gets too hot and dries much faster in plastic. I use old aluminum coffee cans.

12 cup Muffin pan or 3oz. dixie cups. I prefer the muffin pan because the paper is noticeable on dixie cups when tossed into woods or wherever.

Directions:

With vegetable oil grease the pan. If you are using dixie cups, the cups will not come off even if you oil them. Preferred method is muffin pan.

To keep the resin from drying too quick just add your ingredients first then pour resin over the top later. I spray the pan with non-stick cooking spray and then put all the ingredients in each muffin hole, and then pour the resin over the top all at once.

If you are using pennies for extra copper power, place one in the center of muffin hole and add some metal shavings on top of it, the coil and crystals, then a little more shaving on top of that. (If you are using a gallon at a time mixed up you might want to prepare the muffin tins first, the resin can dry and harden before you get to it otherwise). A gallon can make 36-48 OBs.

For the coil, cut off about 6-8 inches of the Copper wire and wrap it around 2 fingers clockwise and slide off placing the coil in center of muffin. Place some copper shavings around the coil, and add 1-2 crystals inside the coil. Looser, wider coils give me more power than tightly wound coils.

I like to put crystals both inside and around the coil.

Fill to 1/3 of top of muffin pan with the ingredients.

Pour resin over. Let it absorb; then pour more resin over it to fill it.

Let it dry. Probably about one hour. Then take out of pan. Let them dry longer.

Make in a well ventilated area, outside or in a garage.

If you are mailing them, wrap them in foil.

Let's get the word out!!

0-595-33559-4

Printed in the United Kingdom
by Lightning Source UK Ltd.
125193UK00001B/452/A